Carlton Holmes Rogers

Incidents of travel in the southern states and Cuba

With a description of the Mammoth Cave

Carlton Holmes Rogers

Incidents of travel in the southern states and Cuba
With a description of the Mammoth Cave

ISBN/EAN: 9783337207632

Printed in Europe, USA, Canada, Australia, Japan

Cover: Foto ©Andreas Hilbeck / pixelio.de

More available books at **www.hansebooks.com**

Incidents of Travel

IN THE

Southern States and Cuba.

WITH A DESCRIPTION OF

The Mammoth Cave.

"A snapper-up of unconsidered trifles."

NEW YORK
R. CRAIGHEAD, PRINTER, 83 CENTRE STREET.
MDCCCLXII.

To

A WIDOWED MOTHER,

A BELOVED WIFE, AND AN ONLY DAUGHTER,

Three Bright Links in Affection's Chain,

THIS VOLUME IS

AFFECTIONATELY DEDICATED.

INTRODUCTORY.

The following pages comprise portions of private letters written by the author to his family during a few months recently spent in Cuba and the Southern States. They are now published at the solicitation of a few friends, who have imagined them sufficiently interesting to warrant their preservation in book form. A limited number of copies have been printed, and as they are intended only for gratuitous distribution among the writer's friends and acquaintances, the "general public" will have little or no interest in the merits or demerits of the volume.

The places visited have so often been described by intelligent travellers that it is almost impossible to avoid occasional similarities in description; yet, as different observers will select different features, or even view the same things differently, it is hoped it will be apparent that the impressions here given, are those received from actual and appreciative observation.

Introductory.

In preparing these letters for the press, some parts of them containing personal allusions (which, like comparisons, are sometimes odious) have been omitted, which will account for the disconnected and fragmentary style of some portions of the work. Those whose tastes incline them to prefer "grave subjects" to those of a humorous nature, may perhaps object to the light and apparently trifling character of some of these letters. Let such remember that variety is the spice of letters, as well as of life, and that

> "A little nonsense now and then,
> Is relished by the wisest men."

This class of readers, doubtless, will find enough that is *heavy* before they finish the volume.

C. H. R.

PALMYRA, 1860.

Contents.

LETTER I.—WASHINGTON.

A City of Magnificent Discrepancies.—Government Buildings.—The Court End.—Presiding *Spirits*.—Habits of the Denizens.—Hotel Life.—A Sudden Illness and Speedy Recovery.—Human Drones.—Levee at the White House, . . 9

LETTER II.—WASHINGTON.

Our National Menagerie.—Fish, Flesh, and *Foul*.—Noble and Ignoble Beasts.—The Lion Rampant.—Scene in the House of Representatives.—A Prosy Member.—A Maiden Speech.—Procuring a Passport.—The Smithsonian Institution.—Washington Monument.—Lions at the Navy Yard, . . . 18

LETTER III.—RICHMOND.

A Picturesque Location.—The Poetry of Nature.—Public Buildings.—Slave Culture.—Climatic Discoveries.—Nondescript Vehicles.—Novel Motive Power.—A Stiff-necked Race.—Past and Present.—Decadence of the Old Dominion.—The F. F. V.'s on the Wane.—Its Representative Statesmen.—Western Virginia.—Its Resources and Future Prospects, . . . 29

LETTER IV.—CHARLESTON.

Tropical Anticipations.—Capricious Weather.—Wilmington.—Staples of North Carolina.—A Moral State.—Slave Gangs.—Our Locomotive Impeded.—An Accident develops an *Incident*.—All's Well that Ends Well.—Arrival at the Palmetto City.—Agreeable Interview with Nature's Sweet Restorer, . 39

Contents.

LETTER V.—CHARLESTON.

Topography of the City.—A Sea-Cybele.—Its Public Parks.—The Athens of the South.—The F. F's and their Peculiarities.—Young South Carolina.—Rice Plantations.—Habits of the Planters.—Suburban Celebrities.—Charleston Harbor and Fortifications.—Physical and Moral Characteristics.—Political Heresies.—Miss Carolina a Lunatic.—A Prophecy. . . 48

LETTER VI.—HAVANA.

First Impressions.—Peculiar Dialect.—National Odor.—The Town of Regla.—Moro Castle.—Fortress of Cabañas —Emancipated Gondolas.—Custom House Ordeal.—Peculiar Registration.—In Pursuit of a Habitation under Difficulties.—The Revere Hotel.—Spanish *Cuisine*.—La Dominica.—A Yankee Room-Mate.—Musical Watchmen, . . . 59

LETTER VII.—HAVANA.

Intra Muros.—Anti-Peripatetic Habits of the Ladies.—Volantes and their Appendages.—Singular Customs of the Cubans.—Narrow Streets—Its Buildings.—Residence of a Marquis.—Ubiquitous Cigar.—Tropical Beauties.—The Cathedral.—Rags and Jewels in close Proximity.—Military Mass, . . 76

LETTER VIII.—HAVANA.

Peculiarities of the Tradesmen.—Mode of Shopping.—Monteros.—Customs of the Milkmen.—Venders of Fruits and Vegetables.—The Pasco de Isabel.—Dazzling Pageant —Plaza de Armas.—The Poor Man's Opera —Tacon Pasco.—The Bishop's Garden.—Fish Market.—Story of Marti the Smuggler, . 91

LETTER IX.—HAVANA.

Visit to the Country.—Guines.—An Unappetizing Discovery.—A John Gilpin Ride —An Ingenio.—Manner of making Sugar.—Congoes and Coolies.—Grades of Society.—Slave Laws of Cuba.—Coffee Plantation.—Tropical Vegetation.—Description of the Trees on the Island.—A Vegetable Phenomenon, . 110

Contents.

PAGE

LETTER X.—HAVANA.

Return to Guines.—A Ludicrous Spectacle.—The Polite Footpad.—Spanish Mode of Robbery.—A Night with the Insects.—A Miserable Posada.—Description of Matanzas.—The Cumbre—Scene in the Cathedral.—Cuban Women Graceful.—The Contradanza and Fandango.—An Evening at Sea.—The Southern Cross.—A Startling Adventure, . . . 134

LETTER XI.—HAVANA.

Domestic Habits of the Cubans—Gambling.—Cock and Bull Fighting.—A Priest-Fearing but not God-Serving People.—Ubiquity of Romanism.—Sabbath in Havana.—An Easter Celebration.—Carrying of the Host.—The Tacon Theatre.—A Spanish *Danseuse.*—My Landlady of the Revere.—Bal Masqué.—A Saturnalia, ... 156

LETTER XII.—HAVANA.

Religious Intolerance.—Protestant Worship Interdicted.—Services on board a British Man-of-War.—A Marine Choir.—U. S. Flag Ship Potomac.—Preaching by a Boston Clergyman.—Closing of Lent.—A Bull Fight.—Private Theatricals.—A Midnight Row on the Bay.—Closing Remarks, . . . 172

LETTER XIII.—KEY WEST.

An Attack of Illness.—Description of the Key of the Gulf.—Coral Insects.—Key Largo.—Amphibious Bipeds.—Wreckers.—Climate, Soil, and Productions of the Island of Key West.—Indigenous Fruits.—Exotic Plants.—Dr. Henry Perrine.—Narrative of the Massacre at Indian Key, ... 189

LETTER XIV.—SAVANNAH.

Sea Voyage.—Old Ocean in Good Humor.—Meet with Friends.—A Starry Night.—Boreas on a Spree.—Personal Experiences.—Objections to Sea Life.—Noticeable Passengers.—A Slave Trader.—A Cosmopolitan and Disciple of Baron Munchausen.—An English Cockney Exquisite.—An Uxorious Husband.—Mated, but not Matched.—An Amusing Finale, 215

LETTER XV.—MONTGOMERY.

Description of Savannah.—The City of Shade and Silence.—Its Monuments.—Laurel Grove Cemetery.—Buonaventura—Georgians Constitutionally and Climatically Indolent.—The Aristocracy of Cottondom.—"Congo" and King Cotton.—Macon.—Columbus.—The Falls of Coweta.—An Indian Legend, ... 228

LETTER XVI.—MONTGOMERY.

Location of the City.—Its Picturesque Suburbs.—Every Paradise has its Serpent.—Decadence of Fogyism.—Ole Bull.—Southern Chivalry.—A Dry Subject.—Cotton the Blood of the State.—Cost of Living at the South.—Southern Staples.—A Northerner's Opinion of Slavery.—Its Objectionable Features.—Talk with a Slave, ... 242

LETTER XVII.—NASHVILLE.

Re enter Georgia.—Natural Productions of the State.—A Georgia Cracker.—Atlanta.—Hotel with an Appetizing Name.—Cool Treatment for Hot Weather.—A Victim.—The Rival Waiters.—Chattanooga.—A Night of Unrest.—Amusing Provincialisms.—Description of Nashville.—Lions of the City.—Its Environs.—Southern Hospitality, . . . 257

LETTER XVIII.—MAMMOTH CAVE, KY.

The Cave Hotel.—Magnitude of the Cave.—Its Population.—Equipments for the Journey.—Atmosphere Pure and Equable.—Body of a Child found.—Hospital for Consumptives.—The Grand Gallery.—Church and Ball Room.—Giant's Coffin.—Goran's Dome.—Bottomless Pit.—The Scotchman's Trap.—Fat Man's Misery.—A Prospective Purgatory.—The Dead Sea.—A Cold Collation.—The Mysterious Bottle.—Gothic Avenue.—Novel Names of Places.—Lover's Leap.—Star Chamber.—Stephen the Guide.—Human Remains found.—River Styx.—Lethe.—Musical Echoes.—Pass of El Ghor.—Perilous Labyrinth.—Cleveland's Avenue.—Croghan's Hall.—Nine Miles from Daylight.—Eyeless Fish.—Piscatory Phenomena.—Conclusion, 275

LETTER I.

WASHINGTON, D. C., *Feb.*, 1856.

IT is customary, I believe, for tourists, and other migratory bipeds, to leave their " tracks in ink;" and from the innumerable books of travel which are scattered over the land, it would seem as if it were imperative on all who wander—*to write*. My tastes are somewhat nomadic, and, although not exactly " a bird of passage," I am " often on the wing." Now, as you are aware, I am on my way to a southern clime, where

> " Milder moons dispense screner light,
> And brighter beauties decorate the night,"—

and if my rambling, desultory letters prove interesting to my family and friends, I shall be satisfied. * * * *

I reached this city two or three days since, in company with our mutual friends Mr. and Mrs. S———, and "put up" at the National Hotel, at the request of the Ex-M. C. who had made that house his home during two Congressional sessions. I shall not attempt to give an elaborate or detailed description of the "Federal Capital," as it would require more time and patience than I have at my command,—but simply to note a few impressions of "men and things" suggested to my mind during my brief sojourn here.

This has been styled "the city of magnificent distances." To me, it appears more like a large, unfinished village, laid out on an extensive scale, and awaiting completion, than a solid, compactly built city of fifty thousand inhabitants. "It is laid out"— to use the grandiloquent language of the guide-book, —"on a plan of great magnitude; and will, if the design of its founders be carried out, and their anticipations realized, be a magnificent memorial of the great man from whom it is named: and a city, whose gigantic proportions shall harmonize with the power and extent of the mighty Republic of which it is the capital."

Washington covers a large extent of territory, and

would be a beautiful city, *if it was finished.* It is extravagant in design, but meagre in execution; pretentious, yet simple; elegant, yet squalid; large, yet small; rich, yet poor. Its design and architecture are abnormal—half city and half village; combining many of the elements of the one, with the appearance of the other. A city in population and extent, but a village in its sparsely built streets, its wide rambling avenues, its low homely buildings, and tiny triangular squares, it has a peculiarly suburban expression. Its private residences, with a few exceptions, are unattractive in appearance, and insignificant when compared with many of the government buildings, which, though in an unfinished state, are colossal structures, magnificent in their proportions, beautiful in design, and noble specimens of American architecture. The Capitol, when completed, will be, without doubt, the finest public edifice in the world. It stands on the brow of a hill some seventy feet above the Potomac, and, from its elevated position, commands a view of the city and surrounding country—a view probably unsurpassed for variety, beauty, and extent, by any in this country.

From the Capitol, which is "the hub" of this political universe, radiate, like spokes in a wheel, various streets and avenues, whose peculiar names comprise most of the letters of the alphabet, many of the numerals, and all of the original States of the Union. Pennsylvania Avenue, the principal thoroughfare, extends in a direct line from the "Capitoline Hill" to the Treasury Buildings, a distance of nearly a mile; there it makes a short *détour*, and continues its course, by the Executive Mansion, to the borders of Georgetown, which is, in fact, but a suburb of Washington. It is a place of but little business, and derives its support entirely from the fashionable denizens of this metropolis. That part of the city where the President's house is situated, is known as "the Court End," where most of the aristocracy who keep house, reside. The best residences are in this vicinity, although but few of them have any pretensions to exterior beauty. The principal hotels, stores, and places of business are on Pennsylvania Avenue, a street of great width and well macadamized, affording a direct and easy communication between the Capitol and the several Departments.

It is an indisputable fact that Washington, during the winter, contains a greater amount of intelligence, vice, beauty, and moral deformity, than any other city in the Union. It is a hibernating place for politicians, office-seekers, fortune-hunters, gamblers, and votaries of fashion and folly. People of almost every rank, color, and nation, are here congregated: and Dignitaries, both civic and military, with titles real or assumed, and persons of known or doubtful reputation, are to be found here "as thick as birds during blackberry time." Governors, senators, generals, colonels, diplomats, envoys ordinary and extraordinary, officers in full-pay, half-pay, and no pay at all, judges of probates and reprobates, members of the bar and frequenters of the bar-room, bankers who preside over the faro-banks and brokers who are always "dead broke," besides a liberal sprinkling of "the fancy," including "men of muscle" and "men of straw." The presiding *spirits* of the place are ardent spirits; the most popular bank the faro-bank; and to be caught "dealing in ivory," is a *capital*, but not an indictable offence. The checks most in use here are "ivory checks," and the dealer is not to be mistaken for "the De'il." To speak paradoxically, those occupying the *highest* positions are often found in the *lowest* places; while those who are always *tight*, are invariably *loose* in their morals. Washington is, in fact, a medley of contradictions. Almost everything appertaining to it is different from what it seems, and nothing is what it appears to be. From the number of hacks and carriages standing in the streets, you would imagine that every one *rode;* yet, from the multitude of pedestrians thronging its avenues, it would appear that every one *walked*. The society is ephemeral, and the city alternately populous and deserted. One month it may be full to overflowing, and the next, presenting a mournful illustration of Goldsmith's "Deserted Village." One set of inhabitants may reside here to-day, and another to-morrow; they are the sport of fortune and politics, and know not whether they are here for a day or for a lifetime.

Washington, though far from being an Eden, is a paradise for hotel-keepers and proprietors of small boarding-houses: who make their hay in the winter, when the sun is not expected to shine. During the summer these places are closed or nearly deserted; grass grows before their doors, which is to be gathered the next winter; thus reversing the usual order of husbandry. These hotels are vast caravansaries—colossal hives, filled with human drones, who subsist on government honey, or prey upon each other. The "B's" hived here are very numerous, consisting, in part, of Benedicts, Bachelors, Belles, Beaux, Black-legs, Blue-stockings, and a miscellaneous collection of "Bugs," big and little. I had supposed that the *big*-bugs were confined chiefly to the White House and the residences of the aristocracy. But I discovered my mistake when I took possession of my room on the upper floor, which was infested with giant cockroaches and other aristocratic insects. How they ever attained such an elevation, through such a labyrinth of passages, and around so many angles, both acute and oblique, was beyond my comprehension, for I was unable to find my way up without the assistance of a guide, after having been once shown the way. But the instinct of animals is sometimes superior to that of the human race. When I first arrived at this hotel, I asked for a quiet room, but did not expect to be sent up into the celestial regions, so far above " this dim spot which men call earth." I retired to rest at the usual hour, and slept soundly until about midnight, when I was awakened by the sound of voices in an adjoining room. At first I supposed them to be students in astronomy. who had sought this elevated place where they could study the *arcana cœlestia* without the aid of a telescope. But I soon discovered, by various noisy demonstrations, that they were votaries of a much less recondite science, although one that is not often investigated without the assistance of *a glass*. These *bon-vivants*, if not believers in spiritualism, were at least *spirit*ually inclined; and if not free-thinkers, they certainly were free-*drinkers*, and kept up their revels until a late hour.

I slept very little that night, and arose the next morning quite indisposed—that is, indisposed to occupy the same room another night. Went down to the office, found Dr. —— (one of the proprietors), to whom I described my symptoms. He pronounced my disease an aggravated *room-attic* complaint, and prescribed as a remedy, " a quiet room on the second floor." I followed his advice, and speedily recovered.

The society in Washington is ostensibly democratic, although there is a sufficient mixture of aristocracy to give it variety. The President is the acknowledged representative of the democracy. His levees are free to all who desire to attend. A coat capacious enough to hide a soiled shirt, a clean collar (or none at all), with a little assurance, is the only passport necessary to executive hospitality. At these semi-monthly reunions, all classes are represented, both plebeian and patrician; the purse-proud millionaire and the penniless vagabond; the foreign count and the native artisan; the stiff upper-crust of society and the lower strata of unwashed and unkempt humanity. A large and promiscuous multitude assemble at the White House on these occasions, to pay their individual respects to the Executive and ruler of this Republican Court.

LETTER II.

WASHINGTON, *Feb.*, 1856.

I HAVE just returned from the Capitol, which might, with propriety, be designated as our national menagerie. During the winter it contains a rare but somewhat antagonistic collection of zoological specimens, consisting of beasts of burden and beasts of prey, birds with beautiful plumage and birds of ill-omen; and another class, interesting to the ichthyological connoisseur, which, from their *scaly* appearance, evidently belong to "the finny tribe,"—that peculiar variety known as "suckers;" but, having been so long out of their native element (although frequently "in hot water"), they would fail to recognise it unless *strongly* diluted. Among the quadrupeds here are the lordly lion, the ferocious tiger, the wily fox, the timorous hare, and "dogs of all degree," from the noble mastiff to the lady's lap-dog and the snarling cur. Conspicuous among "the feathered animals" is the bright-eyed eagle, "who drinks the sunshine, and scales the clouds;" the ghostly owl, shrieking his baneful note; besides an indefinite number of pugnacious game-cocks, gabbling geese, and ignoble turkey-buzzards, who subsist mainly upon government offal. These incongruous quadrupeds and bipeds—both flesh and *foul*, are here in promiscuous confusion; and, to appearance, are much less docile and controllable than that "happy family" of birds and animals on exhibition at Barnum's Museum.

The Senate chamber, to-day, was the scene of an intense excitement. That old senatorial lion from the wilds of Michigan, who had become grey and almost toothless during his long incarceration, was aroused from his lair, and, shaking his hoary mane, roared so loudly as to produce fearful consternation among the lesser animals. It appears that the British lion, which had for so many years been lying "couchant," had, for some unexplained cause, suddenly become "rampant," and was now growling and showing his teeth in anger towards the animals on this side of "the big water;" the news of which had just reached the Federal capital. The doughty Michigander was belligerently inclined. His speech was "full of sound and fury," and signified *something*, if one could judge from the significant looks of the senators, and the breathless attention with which the crowd of spectators in the gallery regarded the speaker, as if they considered his inflammable remarks the harbinger of a conflict with the mother country. I do not, however, anticipate any serious trouble with England. It would be suicidal for her to engage in war with us at this time, and it is the settled policy of our government to maintain peace with all nations.

After having listened for a time to the senator's fiery declamation, and fearing that, if I remained longer, I might become imbued with warlike sentiments, I repaired to the Hall of Representatives, where, as some one has facetiously remarked, "they talk without courtesy, and debate without decency." With equal truth, he might have added, *they chew without moderation, and spit on the carpet without com-*

punction. A more undignified and less orderly assemblage I scarcely ever saw. Some were lounging in their chairs, with their feet elevated upon the desks before them; others were running here and there, or were gathered together in groups, talking loudly, and paying no attention to the "member" who was then speaking: while a large number were at their desks, reading newspapers, writing letters, or tearing their manuscripts into small bits and strewing them over the floor, which was as untidy and *litter-*ary in its appearance as an editor's sanctum. And last, if not least, I observed one gentleman (?) with a rubicund face and a form of aldermanic proportions quietly sleeping in his chair.

After having listened for a while to the speaker who had the floor, and learning that he had been holding forth for nearly an hour, I only wondered that more of the members were not asleep; for a more prosy discourse (I cannot call it a speech) I never before heard. It was "linked *dulness* long drawn out." His methodical manner and monotonous delivery would have been better suited to an itinerant lay-preacher. The gentleman had evidently mistaken his calling. On another occasion, I heard a young neophyte deliver his "maiden speech" before the House; which was the exact counterpart of the one just described. His voice was pleasant, and his manner easy and graceful, but his style was a little too declamatory and flowery for the occasion. At times, he would soar into the regions of fancy,—so high that I trembled lest he would never get back again into this "breathing world." I soon discovered that he was more prolific in words than in ideas; it was *vox et prætereu nihil.* He evidently adhered to the rule of the diplomatic Talleyrand, that "words were not intended to convey, but to conceal ideas." I left during one of his aerial flights, being fearful that some accident might befall him in his efforts to return to terra-firma.   *   *   *

As I design, during my absence, to visit the dominions of Her Catholic Majesty the Queen of Spain, I called to-day at the Department of State, to procure a passport, taking with me a friend to prove my identity—that I was my "individual self," and a native of this land of stars and stripes. Fortunately, I was not obliged to trace my genealogy from the "martyr'd John," whose existence terminated so abruptly at Smithfield; or to show which of the illustrious "ten" had the honor to be my progenitor. But my body-corporeal was inspected longitudinally and latitudinally:—was weighed in a balance, and found not to be *entirely* wanting. For your edification, I will copy a portion of this passport:

"To all to whom these presents shall come, Greeting: I, the undersigned, Secretary of State of the United States of America, hereby request all to whom it may concern, to permit safely and freely to pass Mr. ———, a citizen of the U. S., and in case of need, to give him all lawful aid and protection. Given under my hand and seal, &c." Signed, W. L. Marcy.

Then follows a description of my "outer man." "Stature, five feet ten and a half inches, English measure; weight, one hundred and forty-two pounds; age (I have, I confess, a feminine weakness about exposing my age); forehead, high; eyes, blue; nose, straight; mouth, medium; chin, small; hair, brown; complexion, florid; face, oval." If this is a correct portraiture of my "human face and form divine," it will answer as the descriptive part of an advertisement if I am ever strayed or stolen. As copies of these passports are in all cases made, and preserved in the archives of the department, I shall, hereafter, "live in description," if not "look green in song."

The various public buildings belonging to government, and other objects of interest in and around Washington, have been so often delineated with pen and pencil, that any attempt on my part to describe them would be a profitless undertaking. The most imposing buildings here, aside from the Capitol, are the General Post Office, the Patent Office, or more properly the Department of the Interior, and the Treasury Buildings: all of which are now being enlarged and otherwise improved. They are large and costly structures, and when completed, will be an ornament to this City, and a credit to our Government.

One of the most remarkable buildings here, both on account of its great size and its peculiar architecture, is the Smithsonian Institution, which was erected a short time since, at an expense of over three hundred thousand dollars, by the munificence of a private individual—a foreigner, who had never, that

I could learn, visited this country. In the year eighteen hundred and twenty-eight or nine, an English gentleman of wealth and education, by the name of James Smithson—the supposed illegitimate son of the first Duke of Northumberland—died, bequeathing his entire property, exceeding half a million of dollars, to the United States, for the purpose of establishing in this city an Institution to be devoted to Science, Literature, Art, and every other branch of knowledge by which mankind might be benefited. Congress accepted the bequest, and the money was received into the Treasury in 1838. But several years elapsed before a law was passed for the establishment of the Institution as it now exists. By this delay, the Regents were enabled to erect the present magnificent edifice from the interest which had accrued, leaving the whole amount originally bequeathed, to be applied as expressed in the testator's will.

The building, or rather, series of buildings (for it covers several acres of ground, and looks from a distance like a walled town), is constructed of a reddish-grey sandstone, which is said to be quite soft when it is first quarried, but becomes hard after a short exposure to the atmosphere. The architecture of this building is peculiar. It is a combination of the Gothic, Norman, and other styles of the Feudal ages, and is entirely different from any other structure in this country. Its numerous turrets and towers; its massive walls; its battlemented cornices; its heavy buttresses, and its other mural projections, give it the appearance of great durability, and are suggestive of a grand old castle of the olden-time.

It is surrounded by a highly improved park of about fifty acres, which was laid out by the late A. J. Downing, whose sad death occurred before it was completed. The length of the entire building, including the library, picture-gallery, and laboratory attached, is four hundred and fifty feet. The main building is about one hundred and sixty feet deep, and its wings are of various dimensions. On the first floor is the museum, which occupies a room two hundred feet long, by fifty wide, and twenty five feet high, with a spacious gallery extending round the whole interior. On the floor above is the lecture-room, where lectures on scientific and literary subjects are given during the winter. It is an immense room, capable of seating nearly two thousand persons. The museum contains a large and valuable collection of curiosities from all parts of the globe, which, together with the well stocked library of rare and ancient works, and the extensive gallery of paintings and statuary, are objects of interest to the scholar, the artist, and the antiquarian.

A short distance from here is the celebrated Washington Monument, which, when completed, will be the highest work of art in the world. It is to be six hundred feet high; nearly three times the height of the Bunker Hill Monument, once and a half as high as St. Paul's Cathedral, and more than a hundred feet higher than the great Egyptian Pyramid of Cheops. But appearances indicate that it will be many years before this inchoate memorial of a great, good man, will be finished.

During a brief visit to the Navy Yard on the Potomac, I was shown, by the officer in command, two old French brass field-pieces, whose history is so romantic that I deem it worthy of mention. They were long-eighteen-pounders, exactly alike in every particular, and from the inscriptions upon them it appears that they were both cast at Douay, a city in France, in July, 1740. One, called "Le Vigoreux," came into the possession of our Government during Jefferson's administration, at the time Louisiana was ceded to us by France, and was included in the purchase. The other, "Le Belliqueux," was taken from the Mexicans, at Alvarado, in 1847, and recently brought to this place, where, after a probable separation of more than a century, these twin-messengers of war were reunited, and now stand side by side. Near them were two Spanish brass thirty-two-pounders, which were captured by Captain Stephen Decatur, at Tripoli, in the year 1804.

LETTER III.

Richmond, Va., *Feb.* 1856.

The capital of the "Old Dominion" is distinctively a southern city. It has a population of about thirty-five thousand, and once enjoyed a wide-world celebrity for the wealth, refinement, and high culture of its society. It is situated on James River (formerly known by the more euphonious name of Powaton), a stream of not much magnitude, but of considerable importance to the manufacturing and commercial interests of the city, as it affords a valuable water-power, and is navigable for vessels of small tonnage a distance of nearly a hundred and fifty miles from the ocean.

The city occupies a boldly diversified and beautifully picturesque location. It extends along the steep banks of the river, and over a series of hills, from whose elevated summits the views are singularly varied and beautiful. Its physical aspect and general appearance are said to be somewhat like those of Edinburgh. It has almost as many hills as ancient Rome; but whether it bears any other resemblance to the "Eternal City" I am unable to say. These hills have been designated as the "poetry of Nature." They may be poetical to one who has a carriage always at his command; but if dependent on his own powers of locomotion, he will, I imagine, become so weary by the time he reaches the top, as to be quite insensible to their poetry; such, at least, was my experience.

The finest private residences, and many of the public buildings, are on Shockoe Hill—the aristocratic part of the town—which overlooks the business portion of the city, and commands a fine view of the surrounding country.

The Capitol stands in a public square or park, near which I saw a massive pedestal of granite, waiting to receive an equestrian statue of Washington, by Crawford, not yet completed. The Capitol, from its size and elevated location, is the most conspicuous object in Richmond; and, in the distance, has a noble and classical appearance. A nearer approach, however, disrobes it of that enchantment which *distance* ever lends to the view. It is an imposing looking edifice, of the Anglo-Grecian order of architecture, but, at present, in a state of dilapidation unworthy the first public building in the time-honored and aristocratic state of Virginia. There are many old, distinguished looking residences in Richmond, and several of the streets are broad, and bordered with beautiful trees; yet the city has not a bright and cheerful look. There is an apparent lack of thrift, and a want of paint and complete repair, so essential to the beauty of a place. Notwithstanding these architectural defects, and the questionable morality of the city (which is a hot-bed of slave-culture, where the ebony species are extensively cultivated for market), it possesses many attractions for the northern traveller, and I feel well repaid for my visit.

I observed while here, for the first time since leaving home, indications of the approach of spring, and evidences of my proximity to a warmer zone. Many kinds of half-hardy shrubs and plants had been removed from their hibernal quarters, and were giving evidence of returning life; while the magnolia and other semi-tropical trees, which grow here without protection during the winter, had burst their buds, and were fast becoming clothed with verdure. Observing a tree of singular appearance in one of the streets through which I was passing, I turned to a good-natured, intelligent looking mulatto standing near, and inquired the name. "Why, Massa," said he, respectfully removing his hat and scratching his head, to stir up his ideas, or *something* else; "why, Massa, I disremembers 'zackly his name, but he's a kind of *Heabenly* tree." It proved to be an uncommonly large specimen of the Ailantus, or Tree of Heaven, which I failed to recognise on account of its unusual size.

During my wanderings about the city I discovered many features in animate as well as in inanimate nature, that were peculiarly southern. The general appearance and habits of the colored population, their peculiar dialect, and the nondescript vehicles and appendages used to bring their products to market, were to me quite novel and amusing. Nearly all the carriages that I saw here, even the most pretentious, were oddly constructed, and had an old-fogyish and somewhat dilapidated appearance. Our poorest backwoodsman would not allow his family to appear abroad in as shabby a conveyance as I saw while here, filled with well dressed ladies from the country. The planters generally come to town on horse or mule-back, frequently accompanied by their wives and daughters, who seem to prefer that primitive mode of locomotion. I learn that it is not unusual for the daughters of farmers and planters of small means, to come to the city in a cart drawn by oxen, accompanied by a plantation negro, with his long hickory "gad," who officiates in the double capacity of postillion and beau. After having secured the bovines, and given them their quantum of fodder, he accompanies the ladies on their shopping expedition —a kind of male Duenna, to carry their bundles and keep off the "sparks."

Some of the market-women rode in rude antiquated carts drawn by sleepy-looking donkeys, so small, that no part of them was visible from behind, except the tips of their enormous ears from above, and their quadrupedal extremities below. These tiny creatures make up in strength and endurance what they lack in size, and are valuable for their longevity, and the scanty aliment they require to sustain life. The harness is generally more primitive in its appearance than the vehicle itself, being nothing more than a simple breast-strap with a band across the back to support the thills. The rope traces are often so broken and knotted as to look insecure, and the small cord, substituted for reins, so slender as apparently to be inadequate to guide the stubborn animal. In one of those cumbrous vehicles was an old negro woman perched on a high seat, with her black and wrinkled face half shaded by an enormous calico turban, which crowned her head. She was complacently smoking a corn-cob pipe, and apparently speculating as to the probable quantity of "tea, sugar, and 'baccy" to be procured from the sale of her load of eggs, poultry, and vegetables.

It is no unusual thing to see negro women wheeling hand-barrows in the streets, filled with boxes, wood, and other articles. A strap suspended from their shoulders was fastened to each handle of the barrow, which lessened somewhat the labor; still I could not but think it an unsuitable employment for

A Stiff-Necked Race. 35

women, whether black or white, bond or free. A slightly formed and delicate-looking negro girl passed me in the street, carrying on her head an immense wooden tray loaded with provisions, the weight of which would have dislocated the neck of the most sturdy of the Anglo-Saxon race. But she moved trippingly along, with folded arms and a smiling face, as if unconscious of the weight she sustained, proving conclusively that the descendants of Ham are "a stiff-necked" if not a rebellious race.

While at Richmond, I made the acquaintance of an intelligent New Yorker, who had been a resident of Virginia a number of years, and was familiar with her history, government, and peculiar institutions. He acknowledged, and at the same time lamented, the decadence of the Old Dominion, which, less than half a century ago, was first in rank and the most influential among the original states, while now she occupies but a fifth-rate position among her more numerous sisterhood. The golden age of this Alma-Mater of States has passed away, never more, I fear, to return. She has fallen from her high position, and is no longer "the bright particular star" in our National firmament. A country more eloquent in heroic history, or a society more cultivated and refined than once existed in Richmond, and other populous places in this state, cannot now be found. The high-toned chivalry and unaffected hospitality of Virginians of the olden time has become historical, and is as familiar to us all as household-words. But this "mother of states and statesmen" has wonderfully degenerated. Her brilliancy has become dimmed, and her glory has departed. Where are her illustrious descendants, the worthy representatives of her noble ancestors? Where her heroes, her statesmen, and her orators?—her Washingtons, her Jeffersons, her Madisons, her Henries, and other noble names revered in history, and embalmed in the hearts of their countrymen? Alas! where are they, and on whom have their mantles fallen? Who are now her representative statesmen? Who her heroes and her orators? A Tyler, a Hunter, a Wise, a Prior, and a few other "lesser lights," which are as spots on the sun, when compared with those brilliant luminaries which once shone in our Nation's horizon.

This state no longer sustains the high national, political, and social reputation it once so eminently enjoyed. Her politicians and representative men are wanting in vigor of intellect, stability of character, and many of those moral qualifications so essential to the prosperity and greatness of a state or nation. Her "first families," those belonging to the ancient *régime*, and who boast of a noble lineage, are no longer living in wealth and luxury. Their estates have become decayed and apparently valueless, from want of proper care and cultivation: some have been obliged to sell their best lands, and part with their most valuable family servants, until they have become reduced from princely opulence to comparative indigence; while many of their aristocratic descendants are now living in genteel poverty, with but little left save "the prideful recollections of ancestral name and honors." This is a mournful retrospection, but nevertheless true. * * *

The soil of Virginia, which was once rich and productive, has become impoverished, literally worn out, by unskilful husbandry and the improvident cultivation of tobacco. This is particularly the case in the eastern part of the State, a large portion of which now lies in open uncultivated fields and sterile commons; while Western Virginia, if not advancing with a rapidity equalling that of many of the Northern States, is evidently improving, and with her almost inexhaustible mineral resources, her invigorating climate, and her comparatively productive soil, will continue to improve, if her agriculturists will abandon the cultivation of tobacco and turn their attention to crops that will enrich, rather than exhaust the soil.

Western Virginia has sufficient territory and abundant mineral and agricultural wealth for an independent state; and could she get rid of her improvident " other half," which has long been an incubus on her body-politic, and an impediment to her National prosperity, she would, I opine, soon attain a distinguished position in the sisterhood of States. This is a consummation greatly desired by many of her intelligent citizens, who dislike being subjected to the will and caprice of a class of designing politicians and *quasi*-aristocrats, who control the state, and who evidently care more for political power and personal aggrandizement, than for the prosperity and well-being of her one-and-a-half-million of inhabitants. * * *

LETTER IV.

CHARLESTON, S. C., *March* 1, 1856.

I AM now in the aristocratic and picturesque metropolis of the " Old Carolina State," where I expect to remain until the 4th instant, when I shall take my departure for "La Belle Cuba," as the Cubans lovingly designate their beautiful island. Our staterooms are already secured on board of the steamer Isabel, and in forty-eight hours (health and weather permitting) we shall be gliding over the capricious waters of "the deep, blue sea."

The evening we arrived here was as mild and balmy as a northern June. Overcoats were laid aside, and fires dispensed with. The weather was really delightful, and we enjoyed it the more, having so recently come from the snow-clad and ice-bound regions of the frigid north. But how little do we know what a day or a night will bring forth, or what changes may take place in the temperature, from the setting to the rising of the sun. When I awoke the next morning, it was cold and cheerless; the heavens were clothed in black and weeping piteously. The storm raged without cessation for nearly two days, during which time I remained as closely imprisoned within doors as a leg-chained convict. The weather is now looking more propitious, and Old Sol, by way of encouragement, gives us an occasional glimpse of his bright and ruddy face peering from among the half-threatening clouds which now and then obscure the horizon.

While waiting for Dame Nature to put on a more cheerful aspect, to exchange her tears for smiles, I will give a brief outline of my two days' journey from Richmond to this city. Nothing occurred worthy of mention until we reached Wilmington, the most populous town in North Carolina, where we spent the night. This state does not appear to be in as flourishing a condition as some of the other Southern States. She evidently feels the need of a large commercial city, which would afford a market for her agricultural productions, and a place of shipment for her vast mineral treasures: although her recently constructed railroads have in some measure repaired this deficiency. Her progress has been somewhat retarded by the emigration of her young men, which has impaired the enterprise, but not the virtues of her society. In a moral sense, she is "the noblest Roman" of them all. She owes no debts, and will not incur any.* Her paths are the paths of prudence, if plenty does not always follow in her footsteps. Her people are honest, frugal, and unsophisticated: and if she is deficient in some of the characteristics of her aristocratic but erratic sister, South Carolina, she is less sensitive and meddlesome in her disposition, and has more ennobling qualities of head and heart.

The western portion of North Carolina is mountainous, and not very well adapted to agriculture; but its mountains are rich in minerals, particularly in gold, copper, iron, and coal. The principal agricultural productions of this State are Indian-corn, hemp,

---

* This was the case a few years ago, before she had built any railroads; but, according to the last census, the debt of the state was about $3,000,000.

tobacco, and sweet-potatoes, although many kinds of grain are also grown here to a considerable extent. On some of the low-lands cotton is raised in limited quantities, but by no means as extensively as in the Gulf States, where "cotton is king," and the fleecy product holds dominion and unlimited sway over nearly two millions of her *willing* subjects, and over about as many who are her subjects from *compulsion*, not from choice.

The coast along the eastern part of the State abounds in almost interminable swamps, interspersed with shallow sounds or lagoons. The country a little further inland is sandy and covered with extensive forests of pine, known as "pine barrens," which are appropriately named, as they appear to be *barren* of all vegetable productions except tar, resin, and turpentine. The *modus operandi* of gathering and manufacturing these articles is as follows: A notch is cut in the trunk of the tree near the ground to receive the turpentine as it oozes from the bark which is scarified above. As soon as the cavity becomes full, it is dipped out and deposited in barrels. This process of scarifying is repeated year after year, by extending the incisions higher up the trunk, until the wounded tree dies from exhaustion, when it is cut down and consigned to the tar-kiln. The spirit is extracted from the crude turpentine by distillation, and sent to market in the different forms of resin and spirits of turpentine. There were thousands of barrels of these odorous commodities scattered along the road, and piled up at every station, and for miles around their places of distillation the air was filled with the perfume.

Wilmington is on the Cape Fear river, thirty-four miles from the ocean, and has a population of about ten thousand, including slaves. It is a place of some manufacturing importance, as it contains a number of rice-mills, turpentine distilleries, and machine-shops, besides several large steam saw-mills, which turn out each year between thirty and forty million feet of lumber. Two or three small steamers ply regularly between this city and Charleston, and a number are employed on the river, which is navigable for steamboats to Fayetteville, a distance of one hundred and twenty miles, and for barges and vessels of light draught to the iron and coal regions far into the interior of the State.

We remained at Wilmington but a single night, which, however, was long enough, considering its very indifferent hotel accommodations. The house was quite full when we arrived, which, perhaps, was the reason our party were obliged to occupy such very inferior rooms for the night. After tea I strolled through some of the principal streets, but was far from being favorably impressed with the beauty of the place or the enterprise of the inhabitants. The streets were badly lighted, but sufficiently so to show their imperfect sanitary condition, and to reveal many defects in the arrangement and general appearance of the city.

The next morning we crossed the river to take the cars for Charleston. On the ferry-boat were thirty or forty slaves—men and women, chained together in gangs, and accompanied by their owner or overseer. They were being taken to the slave-mart in this city, to be sold at auction to the highest bidder. It was a sad yet novel sight to me, as it was the first time that I had ever seen these human chattels fettered, and driven like so many animals to market. The women were sad-looking creatures, who seemed to realize to some extent their debased and degraded condition;

but the men had a stolid look, as if devoid of sensibility, and were, to all appearance, as unconcerned and indifferent to their fate, as a flock of sheep on their way to the butcher's shambles.

On the cars we found several agreeable persons from the North, who, like us, were *en route* to the Tropics, in pursuit of health or pleasure. Being all northern men with *northern* principles, we soon became acquainted, and formed a pleasant little *coterie* among ourselves. This was quite fortunate, for us at least, as the country through which we passed was entirely devoid of interest, and the weather anything but pleasant. We had proceeded but a few miles, when our engine (an asthmatic, rickety old concern, which had been used up at the North and sent South to recuperate), began to give evidence of a want of vitality. After several spasmodic efforts at locomotion, it stopped moving, gave a few convulsive shrieks, and yielded up the ghost. Before our patience had become entirely exhausted, we were overtaken by a freight train, which, "like a wounded snake, dragged its slow length along," and propelled us to the next station, where we arrived about midnight, some ten or twelve hours behind time. As the cars that we occupied were to leave on another road, which intersected at this station, the passengers destined for Charleston were obliged to remain there until the arrival of another train the next morning.

The night was not very cold, yet the mercury in our mental thermometer went suddenly down to zero, on being informed that the only lodging-house in that vicinity could not accommodate a dozen persons, while we had here "on deposit," two car-loads of white bipeds, besides a score or two of the descendants of Ham. On reaching the house, we found that there were just beds enough for the ladies of our party and their respective "lords;" consequently the despondent majority began to look about for some place to *horizontalize* during the remainder of the night. A few were fortunate enough to secure two chairs; others, in despair, talked of removing the carpet from the floor to find the softest board upon which to lay their weary bodies. Anticipating the result, I early took possession of a small lounge in the parlor; wrapping my shawl about me, and pillowing my head on my satchel, I tried to compose myself to sleep; but in vain, "the mirth grew fast and furious," and communion with "Nature's sweet restorer, balmy sleep," was out of the question. While debating in my mind what course to pursue, a gentleman of our party came to where I was lying, and informed me *sotto voce*, that there was an unoccupied bed in the room taken by himself and wife, and if I would wait until they had retired, I could come and take possession of it. I gladly accepted the invitation, and notwithstanding the peculiar delicacy of my position, soon wandered off "into the land of dreams." We reached this city the next evening without any further accident or detention, and took rooms at the Charleston Hotel—the Astor of the South; where, for the first time since we left Washington, I have enjoyed the luxury of a good meal, and a night of uninterrupted sleep.

LETTER V.

CHARLESTON, *March* 3, 1856.

I HAVE been occupied the entire day with a resident friend, in familiarizing myself with this city and its environs, and am better fitted for communing with Morpheus, or some other *sleepy individual*, than for holding epistolary converse with absent friends. But the steamer is advertised to leave at six in the morning, and I must write now or not at all.

I am somewhat disappointed in the topography and general appearance of Charleston. Its territory is very much circumscribed, and its narrow streets, with its quaint-looking buildings, impart to it an air of quiet and gloom. Occupying a low, narrow strip of land at the confluence of the Cooper and Ashley rivers, which combine to form its harbor, the city, from a distance, appears as if it was half submerged in water. Like aquatic Venice—

> "Throned on her hundred isles—
> She looks a sea-Cybele, fresh from ocean,
> Rising with her tiara of proud towers."

The streets are generally narrow, but regularly laid out, and bordered with the Pride of India and other semi-tropical trees. The finest private residences here are built of brick, and covered with stucco. They are generally set back some distance from the street, and surrounded by high open verandas, which are covered with vines and creeping plants. I was surprised to see so few public parks within the limits of the city. The only one worth mentioning is the Battery—a broad belt of land, sparsely covered with half-grown shade-trees—which extends for quite a distance along the margin of the bay. Fronting on this promenade are many handsome residences, with spacious gardens attached, belonging to wealthy citizens. The Battery is a favorite resort of the inhabitants during the summer season, especially in the cool of the evening, when the air is laden with invigorating sea-breezes, which are wafted up the bay from the ocean a few miles distant. In another part of the city, near the Military Academy, is a public square of several acres, which is used principally for military parades. Being almost entirely destitute of shade-trees and other natural attractions, it is not a popular resort of the citizens.

Charleston is one of the oldest cities in the Union, and is replete with historical associations and revolutionary reminiscences. It has quite a number of churches, many of them old and unarchitectural; a fine public library; numerous religious charitable associations; a college; a Military Academy, and other institutions, where they "teach the young idea *how to shoot.*" This city, for many years, has been called "the Athens of the South," on account of having produced and fostered so many distinguished statesmen, poets, and philosophers. Its patrician families, those native to the soil, have the reputation of being intelligent, refined, and decidedly aristocratic. They are proud and imperious in their bearing, yet courteous and graceful in their hospitalities, retaining in an eminent degree many of the peculiarities of the

French Huguenots, from whom they are descended. They are, in fact, living types of the ancient *régime*, genuine southerners by birth and feeling, and true representatives of southern society. They have but little taste for commercial or mechanical pursuits, and are not at all imbued with that spirit of progress and go-ahead-ativeness so prevalent at the North. There are many northern men residing here, but southern prejudice, yclept chivalry, is not inclined to yield to northern innovations, or to adopt northern improvements. With them, pure blood is a great desideratum, whether in biped or quadruped, in the human or equine species. They trace their own genealogy back for centuries, and their horses have a pedigree almost as long, and as free from admixture with plebeian blood. It is said, with how much truth I cannot say, that there are more families here of noble lineage, and a greater number of thoroughbred horses, than can be found in any other city in the Union.

The young men belonging to the "first families" here, have the reputation of being refined in their manners, indolent in their habits, but capricious, sensitive, and quick to resent an insult, whether real or imaginary. They are proud of their ancestry, and love to be called South Caro-*lin*-ians, which is their synonym for " pure and undefiled," as they affect to believe everything *plebeian* which does not emanate from the " Palmetto State." Many of them are liberally educated, yet but few are as well versed in useful literature and the sciences as in those *southern* accomplishments

"——of riding, fencing, gunnery,
And how to scale a fortress—or a nunnery."

They are superior horsemen, expert billiard players, capital shots, and well skilled in the use of the short-sword. They are also punctilious as to the rules of etiquette, jealous of their honor, and ready at all times to give or receive satisfaction according to the code of the " duello."

Charleston has long been celebrated for its superior horses and elegant equipages, and I expected to see the streets alive with dashing " turnouts," aristocratic vehicles, and sporting men with fast horses. But I learned, on inquiry, that it was too early in the season for much of an equestrian display. It appears that this city is by far the most populous and gay during the summer, as the aristocracy here reverse the usual custom at the North, of spending the winter in the city, and the summer in the country. Most of the wealthy planters residing within twenty or thirty miles of the city, have residences in town, where they and their families remain during the heat of the summer; for at that time it would not be prudent for any one to remain long on a rice plantation. The land devoted to the cultivation of rice is low, level, and contiguous to some small stream or watercourse, as it is necessary to overflow these rice-fields at certain seasons of the year. This produces a malarious atmosphere, which is almost fatal to the unacclimated. It is deemed extremely hazardous for any white person to remain over night on these plantations during the malaria season, although the negroes are exempt from its deleterious influence.

The country around Charleston is generally too level and monotonous to be really beautiful, yet there are a number of pleasant drives, and many interesting places in the vicinity. On the banks of the Cooper river, two or three miles distant, is the Magnolia Cemetery. This "city of the dead" was once a private estate, bearing the appropriate name of "Magnolia Umbra." It is a quiet, lovely spot, with its mingled woods and waters; its silence and shade; its patriarchal oaks and noble magnolias; its mournful cypresses and fragrant jasmines. Within its sacred precincts, "wrapped in the shades of peaceful quietude," was heard no sound,

"—— no voice
Save what still Nature in her worship breathes,
And that unspoken lore with which the dead
Do commune with the living."

Many of the trees, particularly the cypress, are covered with a species of lichen, or moss, which hangs in graceful festoons from the highest branches, completely shrouding them with its gossamer drapery. This is a singular-looking plant, and is supposed to derive its sustenance chiefly from the air. It has a small, slender stem, not larger than a thread, which is thickly covered with delicate frost-colored leaves, and seems particularly fitted to adorn the trees of cemeteries. Its sombre hue, and waving, pendulum-like motion, as it yields to the slightest breeze, impart to Nature a funereal aspect. This species of lichen is indigenous to this climate, and cannot be made to withstand the severity of our northern winters.

In the vicinity of this city are several places which are interesting on account of the historical associations connected with them. The capacious harbor or bay, extending a distance of some seven miles to the ocean, is strongly fortified, and was the scene of several sanguinary conflicts during the Revolution. Castle Pinckney occupies a shoal about two miles from the city. A little beyond is Fort Sumter, considered by military engineers to be one of the strongest fortifications in the United States. It is built upon an artificial island composed of broken stones and refuse chips of granite from northern quarries. It cost our government half a million of dollars to prepare this island for the present fortification, which will cost as much more when completed. Not far from here is Sullivan's Island, on which stands Fort Moultrie, of Revolutionary fame; although, I believe prior to the Revolution it was known as Fort Sullivan, but changed to Moultrie after the bravery displayed by that officer in defending the city from the British fleet in 1776. This island has become quite a fashionable watering-place, and a popular resort for southerners during the summer. It has a large hotel called the Moultrie House, and is said to rival Newport and Cape May in the beauty and extent of its hard, pebbly beach, and in the superior excellence of its sea-bathing.

I have had but little opportunity, as yet, to study the physical character of the Palmetto State, or to examine into the moral condition of her people. Her political heresies are well known to the world, and her proneness to "sedition, privy conspiracy and rebellion," has sadly tarnished her reputation as a state. Her representative men have evidently paid less attention to her internal improvements, and the development of her vast natural resources, than to "the discussion of political subtleties," and the engendering of intestinal strife and discord between the states. It is a well known fact that this belligerent little state, this hot-bed of secession and nullification, has caused "Uncle Samuel"—that respectable father of thirty-three children, and one in expectancy more trouble and anxiety than all the rest of his numerous family. She is a proud, capricious little bantling, erratic in her disposition, impatient of restraint, and with decided revolutionary proclivities; and furthermore, has made several unsuccessful attempts to break the family compact, and set up house-keeping on her own hook. She has at times exhibited symptoms of lunacy; but a short confinement in a strait-jacket, with a few cooling applications to the brain, according to the Jacksonian mode of treatment, caused a speedy recovery. But she is evidently not in good health, being subject to periodical attacks of dyspepsia—a disease which attacks communities as well as individuals, and is often produced by antagonistic causes; sometimes by too great a flow of bile, and at others by a want of that necessary element in the animal economy. I should not be surprised if Miss Carolina (who is becoming quite advanced in years) should, in a sudden fit of indigestion, commit some rash act, and perhaps wander away from the paternal mansion. But she is too much of a valetudinarian to long take care of herself, and, in all probability, after subsisting for a while on a rice-water diet, with the few crumbs of *discomfort* that she may pick up during her wanderings, she will return, and, like the Prodigal Son, beg to be received again into the family of her paternal ancestor.

But a truce to this metaphor. Time wanes, and I must no longer burn the midnight gas, but try and get a little sleep, preparatory to my early departure in the morning for Cuba's "promised land." The mail this evening brought me letters of introduction from friends in New York to several influential Americans residing in Havana, Matanzas, and Cardenas, which may be of service to me during my visit to those places. My passport has been *viséed* by the Spanish Consul residing here, my ticket procured, stateroom engaged, trunk packed, and I have nothing to do now, but "to wrap the drapery of my couch about me, and lie down to pleasant dreams." * * *

LETTER VI.

HOTEL REVERE, HAVANA, *March* 10, 1856.

I AM at last in Cuba, that "fast-anchored isle," known in Castilian poetry as the Queen of the Antilles; and everything around me appears so novel, so entirely unlike what I have ever seen before, that I can scarcely believe my identity. Havana realizes my idea of an old Moorish town, with its moss-covered turrets, its crumbling walls, its narrow streets, and its oddly constructed buildings of various colors, which have become dimmed by time or exposure, imparting to them a venerable and somewhat dilapidated appearance. As to the inhabitants, I hardly know how to describe them. They are certainly the quaintest, queerest, and in many respects the most *outré* specimens of animated nature that I have ever seen. The language of the lower classes is apparently an admixture of *miserable* Spanish, *more* miserable French, and *most* miserable English. Their speech is rapid, accompanied with vehement gesticulations, and sounds very strange to Anglo-Saxon ears. Pure Castilian undoubtedly is spoken by the higher and better educated classes; but being ignorant of the language, and without the opportunity or inclination to form their acquaintance, I shall not have the pleasure of criticising the purity of their style or the beauty and correctness of their idiom.

My "ideas of society" here are as yet vague and undefined. Images of half-naked negroes, sleek and adipose;—of swarthy officials, redolent of cigar-smoke and garlic;—of huge-wheeled volantes, with liliputian steeds and sable postillions;—of small-sized, thin-visaged señors;—of dark-eyed, plump señoritas;—together with military parades and priestly pageantry, form the impressions most distinctly daguerreotyped on my mind during a three days' residence in this city of one hundred and fifty thousand inhabitants.

We approached this island on the morning of the 7th, just as day was breaking. Our gallant steamer moved slowly towards the mouth of the harbor, awaiting the signal to enter, for no vessels are allowed to pass the Moro between the setting and rising of the sun. As we neared the ramparts, a bright light gilded the eastern horizon, and "Old Sol" slowly emerged from his briny bed, and allowed "the light of his countenance" to illumine the scene before us. The loud roar of a cannon came booming over the water, and instantly, as if touched by the magician's wand, the Spanish flag was unfurled from the lofty tower of Moro Castle. Other flags and signals appeared simultaneously in different parts of the city, apprising the *Habaneros* that an American vessel was approaching.

We passed close to the beetling walls of the castle, whose massive battlements are as grey and old and gloomy as a fortress of feudal times; while the long rows of open-mouthed guns looked down defiantly upon us as we moved silently along in its shadow. On the other side of the entrance, and within gun-shot, stands the small fort of La Punta, which was once strongly fortified, but is now used only as a garrison or prison. The heights beyond the Moro, overlooking the city and harbor, are covered by the extensive fortifications of Cabañas. The massive walls, heavy battlements, and ponderous gates of this fortress give it the appearance, from a distance, of a walled town. It covers an area of several acres, and to garrison it effectively would require at least ten thousand men. It was built during the reign of Charles III., and its cost has been variously estimated at from ten to forty millions of dollars. It is related that this eccentric monarch, on learning the cost of this fortification, called for a telescope and began to survey the heavens. On being asked for an explanation, he remarked, that he was looking for the Cabañas, as a work of such magnitude, and on which so much money had been expended, ought to be visible at a great distance.

The harbor of Havana is said to be one of the largest and best in the world. It is sufficiently deep to float vessels of the largest size, and capacious enough to accommodate the ships of all nations. The entrance is so narrow that only one vessel can come in at a time, and its entire length and breadth are covered by the bristling guns of the Moro and Cabañas. The view as we enter the harbor is beautifully picturesque and peculiarly suggestive of the Orient. On one side is the city, with its long rows of parti-colored buildings, massive and unique in their structure, with their flat tiled roofs, dingy and moss-covered, with here and there a grim grey tower uprising in their midst, imparting to the whole a quaint and Moorish expression. On the opposite side, creeping from the water's edge up the sloping sides of an amphitheatre of hills, is the little town of Regla, once the romantic retreat of pirates and buccaneers, and celebrated for the splendor of its bull-fights. Now it is an uninviting, dilapidated looking place, and remarkable for nothing but its extensive traffic in sugar and molasses. How great the change!—from the chivalry and quixotism of the past to the *dulce et utile* of the present. The heights beyond the town were agreeably diversified with woodland and lawn, with umbrageous trees and verdant herbage; while here and there a majestic palm might be seen lifting its proud head from among the masses of tropical verdure in which it seemed to be imbedded, giving variety and beauty to the scene. The beautiful bay, over whose placid surface we were noiselessly gliding, was covered with vessels from all parts of the civilized world, and with the flags of nearly every nation floating lazily in the breeze.

Our steamer had scarcely dropped its anchor, before we were surrounded by scores of small boats rowed by natives dressed in white, with narrow-brimmed Panama hats surmounting their closely shorn heads, and by real Guinea negroes without hats, shoes, or any outer covering except a *scanty* apology for pantaloons. With uplifted oars, and in a language unintelligible to us, accompanied with ludicrous pantomime, these *barqueros* evidently tried to attract our attention to the merits of their different boats. But our disembarkation was prevented by two sallow-faced Spanish officials "clothed with a little brief authority," and in jacket and trowsers of immaculate purity, who strutted, with cigars in their mouths, before the companion-way to prevent the egress of any of the passengers until their passports had been examined. In about two hours this was accomplished, and our party seated in a boat, surrounded by luggage, and the swarthy oars-men pulling away lustily for the custom-house.

The custom-house reached, our baggage was placed on the stone floor amid a crowd of sallow officials, and stalwart negroes of "the deepest dye." At a given signal, one of these sable Hercules clasped a trunk in his immense arms, and placed it in its required position; the straps were unloosed, the key applied, and in a moment the contents were exposed to view. "A deeply, darkly, beautifully *brown*" individual, with a heavy mustache and a cigar behind his ear, approached, and in a respectful manner made a slight examination of the contents. If no contraband article or death-dealing weapons were discovered, he said *bueno*, and with a wave of his hand the lid fell, and the trunk was safely delivered to the owner, who, however, was not permitted to leave until he had paid the Registrador sixteen reals (about two dollars) and received from him a written permit to remain in the city for thirty days. At the expiration of that time, by the payment of another fee, you can have your permit extended to sixty or ninety days. Should you wish to remain longer on the island, it will be necessary to obtain a letter of domicil, which can be procured through the consul of the country of which the applicant is a native.

This ordeal passed, I breathed more freely. Having purchased the freedom of the city, with the evidence in my pocket, I was at liberty to go where and when I pleased. The streets at the time were swarming with half-naked negroes, creoles, and Spanish soldiers. In sight were a number of rude carts, drawn by sleepy-looking oxen with the yokes fastened to their horns, and numerous ponderous drays, whose motive power was a diminutive horse or mule. We placed our luggage on one of these cumbrous vehicles, and the ladies of our party into *volantes*, with directions to drive to the "Hotel Americana." The gentlemen walked, as the distance was short, and we were all desirous to see as much as possible of this strange-looking city.

We had not proceeded far before we all became sensible of a peculiar odor in the atmosphere, the exact nature of which we could not then determine; but I have since learned that it was the combined odor of garlic and cigar-smoke. The inhabitants use garlic in some form at every meal, and cook it in the open air, and the male population (to say nothing of the females) smoke all the time, except when eating and sleeping; and it is said that many go to bed with a cigar in their mouths, and get up and smoke at intervals during the night. One cannot remain here long without discovering that a cigar is a *sine quâ non* in every Cuban's mouth. It is his *vade mecum*, his nepenthe, his solace in affliction, and the companion of his happier hours. To him, it is not only a luxury, but one of the necessaries of life, as indispensable to his happiness as is the exhilarating souchong to an inhabitant of the Celestial Empire.

At the Hotel Americana we encountered another official, who remained until we had delivered up our permits to the proprietor for safe keeping, and registered our names, places of residence, occupations, ages, and whether benedict or bachelor. This registration, I understand, is required of all foreigners who visit this island, so that the record here made, may be compared with their passports, which are retained by the authorities until the owner wishes to leave, when it is given up, and another fee of four or five dollars exacted, compelling us to pay an *export* as well as an *import* duty.

This hotel being nearly full when we arrived, Mr. Wolcott the proprietor was able to accommodate but a few of our party, and they had to take up with miserable rooms. After breakfast I went out in search of other quarters. Every *posáda* that I visited, was full, or the rooms so very uncomfortable that I would not engage them, and I was about giving up in despair, when I met an American friend who was stopping at the Hotel Revere. I returned with him, and secured a room, or part of a room, at that hotel, the apartments being so large that two or three, and sometimes a greater number of persons occupy the same room. I was glad to find accommodations anywhere, for I was tired of wandering about this strange city, with its confusion of tongues, in pursuit of "a local habitation." My morning's experience had taught me the folly of being super-fastidious, and I made up my mind to be satisfied with such accommodations as I could get. I was disposed to adopt the language of the philosophic Touchstone in the play of "As you Like it," and mentally exclaimed, "Ay, now am I in *Cuba?* The more fool I. When I was at home, I was in a better place; but travellers must be content."

The Hotel Revere is much larger than Wolcott's, but was not well kept. The rooms are more capacious and better ventilated, but its larder is not as well stocked, and the *cuisine* is more exclusively Spanish. The table is not such as would be tolerated in our country, as nearly all the viands are badly cooked, and *taste* as well as "smell of Havana." The butter is not only odious, but *odorous;* I smelt it once, and ever since have had it removed as far from my olfactory organs as possible. I have no desire to repeat the experiment. Most of the food is particularly unsavory to me, as garlic is an ingredient of nearly every dish. The meats are evidently cooked in rancid butter or grease, and many of the vegetables fried or compounded with something that renders them extremely unpalatable. Their bread—a kind of French twist—is excellent; consequently, I lean upon *that* "staff of life," assisted by a few other edibles, such as eggs, fried plantains, and sweet-potatoes, with a dessert of tropical fruit. As a beverage, I use water, and a light, sour native wine, which, though not very delicious, is infinitely more palatable to me than their coffee or tea. Good coffee and chocolate can, however, be obtained at some of the restaurants, and several of our boarders, who are extravagantly fond of these beverages, take their matutinal meal at the Dominica, a popular restaurant near by.

La Dominica is on the Plaza, near the captain-general's residence, and is the fashionable lounging-place for citizens as well as strangers. A crowd of people, representatives of many different nations, assemble here during the evening to smoke their cigars and to discuss the news of the day over a cooling sherbet, or some of the delicious ices for which this place is celebrated. As early as nine o'clock all the marble tables are occupied, and so many different languages spoken by the occupants that a sort of Babel-like confusion reigns. The waiters respond to your signals with alacrity, and if you have learnt enough Spanish to make your wants known, you will be served immediately. If you wish to light your cigar, you have but to ejaculate "*candéla!*" (fire), and a servant is at your elbow with a small silver brasier containing live-coals, which he places on the marble table before you, and departs to execute some other order. As the evening wanes the air becomes strongly impregnated with the odor of cigars, which might be disagreeable to those not partial to the narcotic perfume, were it not that the spray from a tiny fountain in the room is diffused through the cigar-scented atmosphere, purifying and rendering it delightfully cool and agreeable. Costa and Co., the proprietors of this *Café*, deal extensively in conserves and sweetmeats; their guava jellies and marmalades are nicely put up in boxes for exportation, and sent to all parts of Europe and the United States.

I learn on inquiry that nearly every article of consumption, with the exception of sugars, cigars, and tropical fruits, is dearer here than with us. Beef, mutton, and pork, are about twenty-five cents a pound. Fish and fowls are equally dear, especially in Havana; the first being a government monopoly, and the supply of the other not being equal to the demand. The duty on foreign flour is so great as to be almost equivalent to a prohibition; nearly all that is used here comes from the mother country, and is exorbitantly high. The price of board at the different hotels in Havana is from three to four dollars a day. So far as my experience goes, the fare and accommodations are execrable; and were payment refused, a valid defence would be *no value received*.

The Hotel Revere, as some one has quaintly remarked, is in appearance a Moorish palace, in discomfort a German boarding-house, in expense a Bond street hotel. It was once the private residence of the Marquis de Cardénas, a wealthy Spanish nobleman, who lived here for a time in almost regal splendor; but he became dissipated, squandered his property, and was finally obliged to give up this establishment. It is now held by the Captain-General, who is the ostensible owner, although it is said that the rents go to the support of the marquis, who is still living. I occupy a large double-bedded room with one immense window opening into the street, from the balcony of which I can almost pluck the rich golden oranges from the well-filled panniers of the vender of fruit, as he rides along the narrow street beneath perched on the rump of his patient mule. Dropping a *real* (a shilling) into the extended hand of the dealer, I am the grateful recipient of a hatful of this delicious tropical fruit for my early-morning repast.

My room-mate is a veritable Yankee, from the lumber district of Maine, who is here negotiating the sale of several cargoes of sugar hogsheads and boxes manufactured in that State. He is quite an agreeable companion, and decidedly an acquisition to *my* society, possessing as he does a fund of good-humor and good sense, and speaking "broken Spanish" sufficiently well to be my interpreter when required. He is well "posted" in politics, pine-lumber, and cigars. As a connoisseur of "the weed," he prefers that grown on a certain plantation in the Abajo district, and pronounces Cabana's celebrated two-hundred-and-fifty-dollars a thousand cigars an expensive humbug, and only purchased by "fools of quality," and those having more money than brains. These high-priced cigars are called Napoleons, and are purchased only by foreigners, who are not generally aware that in Cuba the price of an article is not always regulated by the quality. These cigars are about six inches long, uniform in size, and as perfect in shape as if they were turned in a lathe. In quality, they are but little, if any, better than some brands that can be purchased for sixty dollars. The quantity of tobacco used in their manufacture, and the care necessary in selecting and preparing the outside wrappers—which are all of a color and free from imperfections—are the reasons assigned for the extravagant price asked for them. A gold medal was awarded to Cabana for the best cigars exhibited at the last Paris exhibition; since which time his orders from Europe have increased to such an extent, notwithstanding his exorbitant prices, that he is rapidly accumulating a fortune.

The few days that I have been here have passed very pleasantly, as most of my time is occupied in sight-seeing; but the nights are not without their discomforts and annoyances. The ill arranged mosquito bar attached to my cot does not entirely exclude those phlebotomizing insects; and the window being destitute of glass and shutters, there is nothing to keep out the " voices of the night," which at times are not very somnus-inspiring. The clocks of the neighboring churches strike quarter-hourly, and as the sound dies away, the watchmen in the streets (and there is one stationed under my window), with a shrill, lugubrious cry, announce the hour. This peculiar cry, so distinct and ear-piercing, seriously disturbs my slumbers; but I presume that as I become more accustomed to the sound, it will be less annoying. These "guardians of the night" are called *serénos*. They carry with them a lantern, a long spear, and a brace of pistols, and cry the time of night with a prolonged musical repetition of the syllables, usually commencing with the name of the Holy Virgin, and ending with the word *seréno-o-o* long drawn out, to let the sleepers know how quiet and serene are the heavens above them. *Seréno* is a Spanish word, and belongs to two different parts of speech, each having a distinct and different signification. When used as a substantive, it signifies a night-watch, while the literal interpretation of the adjective, is quiet, mild, serene. * * *

LETTER VII.

HAVANA, *March*, 1856.

It is now about two weeks since I first landed upon these shores, and during that brief period I have seen so much, have witnessed so many strange scenes, that I can hardly realize that so short a time has elapsed. It has been an eventful fortnight to me, as well as an industrious one; for I have devoted all of my available time to sight-seeing, and have accomplished as much already as most tourists would during an entire season.

In my last letter, I gave a brief description of the harbor of Havana, its fortifications and defences, together with my first impressions of the city and its inhabitants. These impressions were of course desultory, being formed from a limited acquaintance with a few of the principal streets *intra muros* (within the walls). Since that time I have become familiar with the entire city from *Costa del Norte* to the extreme southern limits; and from the waters of the *Bahia de la Habana* on the east, to the crowning heights of "Castle Principe" on the west. I have seen the city in all its phases: at break of day, in the heat and glare of a meridian sun, at dusky twilight, and in the full blaze of gas-light; have lost my way while wandering through its labyrinthine streets, and had a narrow escape from a douche and "a flowing sea," while clambering over the rocky beach at the base of La Punta, in search of shells and specimens.

The city proper contains about one third of the entire population, and is separated from the suburbs by a high wall and moat, which extends, in an elliptical course, from the mouth of the harbor to the southern limits of the bay. At the terminus of several of the principal streets are enormous gateways guarded by Spanish soldiers, whose duty it is to challenge all strangers who pass through. But I repeatedly passed and repassed without being challenged, or even noticed by the automatic sentinels, who are evidently stationed there more for military display than for real service.

The streets of the city within the walls are so narrow and the houses built so close to them, that they have more the appearance of private lanes than highways for travel. Though they are only wide enough to allow two carriages to pass each other, and to a stranger that would seem a hazardous undertaking, collisions are of rare occurrence. On each side of the street are narrow flaggings of stone for pedestrians : but sidewalks are of little use in this city, as but few of the inhabitants ever walk. The "spinning of street-yarn," a practice so much in vogue among the peripatetic ladies of the north, is a decidedly unfashionable pastime here, only indulged in by foreigners and natives of the poorest class. The Cuban gentlemen *seldom* walk, the ladies *never*, except during some of the Holy-days, when carriages are not allowed on the streets.

The vehicles used here are called "Volantes," and are peculiar to this country. In shape and appearance they bear some resemblance to our old-fashioned one-horse chaise, except that the wheels of a volante are considerably larger, and the shafts more flexible and nearly twice as long. The "propelling power" (a small native horse or mule) is at least six feet from the body of the carriage, which is hung midway between the horse and the axle, imparting to it an elastic and cradle-like motion. The horse is ridden by a negro called a *Calesero*, who is usually dressed in fanciful livery, with immense jack-boots reaching far above his knees, and his *sombrero* (if he is fortunate enough to own one) is generally ornamented with bits of gay ribbon, or a feather plucked from the tail of some domestic fowl or bird. A few of the more pretentious volantes have two horses, one for the postillion to ride while guiding the other which is attached to the carriage. This is certainly a humane and *horse-pitiable* procedure, for it is enough that the poor little animal is compelled to draw a heavy volante containing two or three persons, on a full gallop, without being encumbered with a heavy pack-saddle and a clumsy postillion. The long tails of the horses are braided and fastened to the pommel of the saddle, it being considered ornamental. It is at the same time a useful precaution, as it prevents those mercurial appendages from whisking the faces of the few pedestrians they may encounter in the narrow streets. The sidewalks are so narrow that, when two persons meet, one is obliged to step into the street, and in so doing must keep a sharp look-out to avoid the danger of being brushed against by the passing volantes.

But few of the shops and private residences here are above one story high; none that I have seen are more than two. The rooms are large and of great height. In buildings of one story they generally extend to the rafters, which are painted some bright color and left exposed to view. There is but one door in front, which is sufficiently large to admit the passage of a volante with its horse and rider. The carriage is usually left near the entrance, and is visible from the street; while the horse is taken to an open court in the rear, which is used as a kitchen and stable conjointly. Among the middle classes the volante is often seen occupying a place in the best room in the house; for it is here considered an indispensable appendage to every household, and its possession is a more certain passport to Cuban "upper-ten-dom" than would be the occupancy of "a fourstory brown stone front" in the fashionable *purlieus* of Fifth Avenue. Some of the most opulent families have half-a-dozen or more volantes, one for each marriageable daughter. The greater the number and the more expensive the equipages the higher the owner rises in the scale of respectability. Many persons in straitened circumstances, it is said, practise the most rigid economy, and even debar themselves from many of the luxuries of life, to enable them to keep a volante and its necessary accompaniments. It is a national weakness which pervades all classes of society from the titled millionaire to the humble artisan.

Nearly all the buildings here have a venerable, and, in the distance, a somewhat dilapidated appearance. They are mostly built of stone covered with a species of stucco, and colored to suit the taste of the owner or occupant. One story may be blue, the other yellow or green, and the next building just the reverse. This bright and somewhat incongruous combination of colors would be apt to produce a dazzling and unpleasant effect on the eye were it not that the climate and the proximity of the ocean soon destroy the lustre of the paint, and impart to the buildings a faded and time-worn appearance. In buildings of two stories, the first floor is generally used as a shop or warehouse, and in some instances as a stable, while the floor above is occupied as a hotel or private residence. Many of the wealthy merchants here live and do business under the same roof. The first story of the Captain-General's Palace, on the Plaza, is now occupied by shop-keepers, and you can buy a cup of coffee and a cigar in a saloon under the drawing-room of her Excellency Madame Concha, or have your horse shod or your own shoes repaired beneath the roof of some of the most aristocratic of the Cuban nobility.

A brief description of the Hotel Revere, which was once the residence of a Spanish nobleman, will give some idea of the construction and arrangement of the best buildings in Havana. It is two stories high, with a plain, unpretending façade, and only distinguishable from some of the adjacent buildings by its numerous balconied windows on the second floor. The only entrance from the street is through a capacious doorway, almost large enough to admit two carriages

A Nobleman's Residence. 83

abreast. Its ponderous double doors studded with innumerable bolts of iron, and otherwise rendered burglar-proof, are seldom closed except at night. Within this doorway you will commonly see one or more volantes, also the bed and table of the porter, who remains there night and day. He is usually engaged during the intervals between sleeping and eating in making cigarettos, repairing garments, or some other light mechanical occupation. At the further end of this hall, or passage, is an open court, where you will find the atmosphere impregnated with a peculiar odor. Olfactory organs naturally acute, with nice powers of discrimination, will soon discover it to be a combination of garlic, cigar-smoke, and offal. I will here say in explanation, that within this area of a few square rods several horses are stabled at night and during the heat of the day. Near by, and within smelling distance, is the kitchen and culinary department, where garlic is cooked at least twice a day, and is an ingredient in nearly every dish set upon the table. While here, there, and everywhere, may be seen the smoke arising from the ubiquitous cigar, in the mouths of landlord, guest, cook, scullion, and groom; for everything here pertaining to humanity, whether it be high or low, rich or poor, bond or free, is, to some extent, a consumer of the universal " weed."

We next ascend a broad flight of stone steps to a long open corridor or gallery, which is used as a dining-room and public promenade. At one end of this corridor is the parlor, at the other the kitchen; and between the two, at regular intervals, are doors leading to the principal apartments, which are used as lodging-rooms, and now occupied by guests. These rooms all open into each other, and are large, airy, and would be very pleasant were they not so poorly furnished. A small cot-bedstead in each corner of the room, a tiny wash-stand, and two or three cane-bottomed chairs, are about all the furniture they contain. The floors are of tile, with a small bit of carpet spread by the side of each cot, the heat of the climate rendering wooden floors and carpets uncomfortable. The rooms below us, on the ground floor, are used as shops and warehouses, and have no communication in any way with this hotel.

In buildings of one story, the windows are generally about half the size of the room, and nearly on a level with the street, for the purpose of admitting as much air as possible. In the place of sash and glass are heavy iron gratings, which give to the building very much the appearance of a prison. Usually there are light curtains or wooden shutters on the inside, but these being seldom closed, the living room and family group are visible to the passer-by, who is at liberty to stop and gaze within as long as he chooses, without exciting notice or remark from the occupants. In fact, the Cuban ladies seem to be rather flattered than otherwise by such attentions from strangers, which they construe into evidences of admiration.

Much has been said and written of an extravagant nature about the beauty of the Cuban ladies. They *are* beautiful, if dark, dreamy eyes, luxuriant hair, and magnificent busts *alone* constitute beauty. But I confess my disappointment in these Creole beauties—these tropical houris, whose praises have so often been celebrated in poesy and in song. Theirs is an *external* beauty—the perfection of form and feature, without the charm of modesty and refinement, qualities so essential in the female character. Vanity is evidently one of their petty foibles, and coquetry one of their most prominent characteristics; and nowhere is there a better opportunity for displaying these peculiar traits than in church. When in the act of kneeling, many of them take especial pains to arrange their dresses becomingly, and place their jewelled hands where they will show to the best possible advantage; and when apparently absorbed in their devotions, you will occasionally see one plying the telegraphic fan, or exchanging tokens of recognition with some favorite señor in another part of the building. It is a noticeable fact that the Cuban ladies have the art of wielding the fan with a grace and dexterity unsurpassed by any nation in the world. They are initiated into its coquettish mysteries during their youth, and, when they are grown up, it becomes in their hands the very perfection of acting, and the language they impart to its use is an expressive pantomime that requires no interpretation.

Among the many churches and other public buildings in this papal city, none have more interesting associations connected with them than the cathedral, a large and oddly constructed building, whose massive walls and turrets are grey with age and crumbling with decay. Within this venerable church repose the remains of the great discoverer, Christopher Columbus. The coffin containing his revered ashes is inclosed in the wall near one of the principal altars, and the chain with which an ungrateful monarch once bound him, is said to be preserved here, but is not shown to visitors. Among the paintings in this church, is one representing the solemn celebration of the mass previous to the departure of Columbus on his first expedition in search of a new world. Many of the paintings are quite large, and are said to be the productions of the old masters; but they were suspended so high on the walls, that I was unable, on account of near-sightedness, to give them a critical examination.

As the cathedral is not far distant from my hotel, and is open at all hours of the day, I visit it quite often. The music is sometimes exceedingly fine, and some of the services quite impressive; but many of the forms and ceremonies are so senseless and apparently *soulless*, and the pageantry so extremely ridiculous, that it cannot fail to excite in the bosom of every true Protestant mingled feelings of pity and disgust. The congregation is usually composed of all grades, colors, and sexes; but a majority are ladies, apparently of the best classes, who assume the most devout attitudes, and remain the longest time at their devotions. Many of the men (particularly among the laboring classes) merely come within the door, drop on one knee, with their faces turned towards the principal altar, and utter a short, but scarcely audible prayer. When this is finished, they dip a finger in the consecrated water, make a sign of the cross on their foreheads, and glide out as noiselessly as they came in. None of the churches that I have visited contain any pews, and only an occasional seat near the wall; so that all who come there to worship must kneel or stand. It is a beautiful sight to see several hundred señoras and señoritas kneeling or half reclining on showy mats or bits of gay carpet, their necks and arms bare, and often resplendent with jewels; their dark glossy hair ornamented with pearls or flowers, and their exquisitely wrought fans, inlaid with gold and precious stones, "glittering in their hands like so many butterflies."

Each lady, as she enters the church, is accompanied by her sable *calesero*, or footman, carrying in his arms a rich rug or elaborately embroidered stool, for his mistress to kneel or sit upon; and he usually remains standing or kneeling by her side during the service. Soon, mendicant women, old, decrepid, and of all colors, crowd their way in and kneel among the interstices of the richly rugged floor, apparently without annoyance to their fair neighbors. There were black and white, old and young, rich and poor, bond and free, all kneeling side by side. I was, I must confess, considerably surprised at this apparent willingness of these high-born dames to amalgamate with those of low degree. It is true, we are promised such things *hereafter;* but this bringing of rags and jewels—the lustre of ebony and the brilliancy of pearl—into such close proximity *here below*, is more than was ever "dreamed of in my philosophy," and something that I did not suppose would ever occur in this world of sinful fastidiousness. Military mass is celebrated in some of the churches every morning at six o'clock, and one or more companies of soldiers, with their officers, are always in attendance. It is a curious sight to see one or two hundred soldiers, with bristling bayonets and gleaming swords, come marching into church to the tap of the drum, and array themselves in "serried files" as if with hostile intent. But there is nothing in their manner to inspire the spectator with devotional feelings. They go through all the multifarious forms and ceremonies with a kind of automatic precision, as if they regarded it as a military rather than a religious duty.

LETTER VIII.

HAVANA, *March*, 1856.

THE Habaneros are a peculiar people. Many of their habits and customs are entirely different from ours. The tradesmen seldom place their names over their shop doors, but adopt a sign either poetical or fanciful, such as "La Favorita," "La Moda," "El Sol," "Belle de Cuba." Sometimes they are more ludicrous than poetical. For instance, " El Póbre Diablo" (the poor devil) is the name of a popular dry-goods store in the *Calle del Obispo*. The Cuban ladies usually make their purchases in the morning, or just previous to their evening drive on the *Paséo*. They never leave their volantes, but have such articles as they wish to examine brought to them by the shop-keeper or his clerks, it being considered as direct a violation of the established rules of etiquette for a 'lady to enter a store, as to be seen walking the streets. Many of the ladies here do their shopping without leaving their homes. On sending word to a store, a clerk is despatched to the lady's residence with a basket containing such goods as she may wish to examine. If the customer is not suited, the clerk will go to all the principal stores in the city, and procure, if possible, the article desired. Some of the merchants send each morning to the principal hotels samples of their most attractive goods for the inspection of the lady boarders, who can, if they choose, make their purchases without leaving the hotel. This is appreciated by those who are disposed to conform to Cuban etiquette; but most of the American ladies, I observe, are so unfashionable, as to prefer to do their own shopping.

A singular custom prevails among the milk-men here, as well as in other large towns of Cuba, in their mode of supplying the inhabitants with the lacteal beverage. They drive their cows and goats through the streets at an early hour in the morning, to be milked at the doors of their customers, giving to each the quantity required for the day, warm and free from adulteration. When all their customers are supplied, the patient animals are driven home, or turned out to pasture among the mountains. This compulsory itinerancy, and the habit of extracting a limited quantity of milk at a sitting, has an injurious effect on the cows, and they cease to "give down" their milk freely under this treatment.

The vender of fruit, vegetables, and other domestic products, brings his supplies to market in large straw or willow-panniers slung across the back of his sleepy donkey, whose owner is often seen perched upon the rump behind. He rides close up to the windows of the houses, to give the mistress or domestic of the establishment an opportunity to examine his "stock in trade" without their going out of doors. It is not unusual for a farmer from the mountain districts to come to town with a dozen horses or mules fastened together one before the other, and loaded with provender. The horses are tied each to the tail of the one preceding it, and their mouths muzzled so that they cannot filch from their predecessor's load, which is in such tempting proximity. The diminutive animals are often so completely hidden under immense bundles of straw, or the green leaves of Indian corn —which is used here principally as fodder—that they look like so many "walking stacks," and in the distance present a novel and somewhat ludicrous appearance. The horseman who leads the cavalcade usually wears a high pointed sombrero, enormous spurs upon his heels, and sometimes carries a sword and pistols by his side. The latter are evidently worn more for ornament than use, as these *Monteros* are as fond of show and as eccentric in their tastes, as some of the old Spanish hidalgos from whom they *may* have descended.   *   *   *

Havana is evidently a place of considerable business, yet to visit its public promenades and places of amusement, one would suppose all the inhabitants were sybarites, and that business was secondary to pleasure. In the morning, before the heat becomes oppressive, these places are frequented; and when the sun is low down in the horizon, every street and avenue becomes filled with gay and expensive equipages, on their way to the Paséo de Isabel, the fashionable drive and promenade *estra muros* (beyond the walls). Passing out at the Monserrate gate through an arched gateway guarded by stupid sentinels, and over a deep moat, you reach this celebrated avenue, where all the wealth, fashion, and beauty of the city do congregate. This Paséo extends in a direct line from the Prado to the *Campo del Marte*, or military square, a distance of nearly a mile. It is about four hundred feet wide, and consists of five separate drives, running parallel with each other, which are bordered with fine trees and ornamented with fountains and statues. As the day begins to wane, and the heat-laden air gives place to soft ocean breezes, this avenue becomes the scene of indescribable gaiety. The numerous walks are thronged with pedestrians; countless numbers of volantes, freighted with their precious burdens, pass and repass each other in rapid succession, and one not accustomed to such a scene, gazes until his sight becomes dazzled and his senses bewildered by so much splendor and magnificence.

This pageant is kept up until about eight o'clock, when the Paséo becomes deserted by the fashionables, who repair to the *Plaza de Armas*, where some of the fine military bands play for an hour every evening. This gratuitous performance is called by the Cubans "the poor-man's opera," and is extensively *patronized* by all classes. The various walks in the Plaza are thronged with pedestrians, and the streets surrounding it filled with volantes; the fair occupants being engaged in "discussing" a vanilla-ice or cooling sherbet, from La Dominica, a popular restaurant near by; or in coquetting with some familiar acquaintance, who may have approached their carriage during the pauses of the music. In the midst of this gay crowd may be seen Spanish soldiers, with their bayonets glittering in the bright moonlight, who are stationed here, as well as in all other parts of the city, to remind the people, that not only during war, but in peace and while engaged in innocent recreations, they are under the control of a military force that is omnipresent and all-powerful. * * *

Since writing you last, I have become somewhat familiar with the environs of Havana, and have spent many pleasant hours upon the green sloping hills which lie adjacent to the city. Castle Principe stands upon one of the highest elevations, and the view from its massive battlements is one of the finest that I ever witnessed. The city and its suburbs lie, as it

The Bishop's Garden.

were, almost at its very feet; and the land-locked bay with its myriads of vessels sleeping on the tide, as well as the crescent-shaped hills beyond, covered with perennial foliage, are distinctly visible from this elevation, and form a living picture on which the eye delights to linger. A pleasant drive is through the Tacon Paséo (over a road as smooth as a pebbly beach, and lined on each side with double rows of giant palms) to that romantic suburb known as the Cerro, with its quaint little villas and unpretentious cottages overburdened with shade, and redolent of the perfume of flowers. Not far from here is the celebrated "Bishop's Garden;" so called, from its once being the residence of the Bishop of Havana. It is now uninhabited, and everything about it going to decay. The house itself is but a moss-covered ruin, its roof having been torn off by a hurricane which nearly devastated the island a few years since; and its crumbling walls of stone and stucco are covered with moss and parasitical plants. The walks about the grounds are now choked with weeds; the fish-ponds are filled with stagnant water, and uninhabited, except by frogs and slimy reptiles; the bridges are decayed; its marble statues broken or displaced, and covered with a gangrenous mould, and everything appertaining to the place has the appearance of desolation and decay. The only person that I saw on the premises was a solitary laborer, who was engaged in cultivating a few vegetables for the Havana market.

Nothing that I have yet seen in this city has interested me more than the *Pescadéria* or fish-market; and I would advise those who have a taste for ichthyological æsthetics, or a curiosity to witness eccentric combinations of colors, if they ever come to Havana, not to fail to visit this interesting, yet somewhat *scaly* institution. The long rows of marble counters, extending as far as the eye can reach, are covered every morning with bright and shining heaps of these " treasures of the deep," which rival in lustre the brightest shells of the ocean, and, in variety of shade and intensity of color, the very rainbow itself. It is supposed by some, that the peculiar richness and variety of color displayed by these piscatory phenomena, are imparted to them by the sun when he casts his prismatic bow into the briny deep. This theory is sustained by the interesting fact that the multitudinous tints and variegated hues of the rainbow are here exhibited with wonderful distinctness. Every conceivable color and shade is to be seen here, from the most vivid scarlet and brightest orange, to the softest azure and the palest green. Incomprehensible nature, in her moments of caprice, has strangely blended and mixed these various colors, forming grotesque and fanciful pictures for the eye to rest upon. One side of a fish may be blue, and the other a bright scarlet or orange. Another, perhaps, has a crimson back, green sides, and a blue head or tail beautifully flecked or shaded with orange. Others are covered with spots or stripes of various hues, or fantastically variegated; and some look, a short distance off, as if their sides were composed of layers of silver and gold, alternating and lapping over each other. It was certainly a curious sight, and more than realized my expectations. Notwithstanding the waters in the vicinity swarm with the "finny tribe," and the markets are abundantly supplied, this species of food is exceedingly dear. This arises from the fact of its being a government monopoly, and none but its agents are allowed to take fish from these waters, or to offer them for sale in this city.

An interesting story is told concerning this monopoly, which is so romantic that I shall relate it. A quarter of a century ago the coast of Cuba was infested by a band of smugglers and semi-pirates, commanded by "a bold bad man" named Marti, who was known as the "King of the Isle of Pines," a cluster of small islands in the vicinity, where he made his head-quarters, and whence he sent his small, fleet vessels out on marauding expeditions. When Tacon first became governor-general of Cuba (about the year 1834), finding that the revenues of the island had become very much diminished from the extensive smuggling upon the coast, he determined, if possible, to put a stop to the nefarious practice. The entire available maritime force was called into requisition, and armed vessels coasted night and day for months, without the least success against the smugglers. At last, finding that all his expeditions against them failed,* partly from the adroitness and bravery of the smugglers, and partly from the want of pilots among the shoals

* See Ballou's History of Cuba.

and rocks that they frequented, a large and tempting reward was offered to any one who would desert from his comrades and act in this capacity in behalf of the government. At the same time, a double sum, most princely in amount, was offered for the person of Marti the leader, dead or live. These rewards were freely promulgated, and posted so as to reach the ears and eyes of those whom they concerned; but even these seemed to produce no effect, and the government officers were at a loss how to proceed in the matter.

"It was a dark, cloudy night in Havana, some three or four months subsequent to the issuing of these placards announcing the reward as referred to, when two sentinels were pacing backwards and forwards before the main entrance to the governor's palace, just opposite the grand plaza. A little before midnight, a man, wrapped in a cloak, was watching them from behind the statue of Ferdinand, near the fountain; and, after observing that the two soldiers acting as sentinels paced their brief walk so as to meet each other, and then turn their backs as they separated, leaving a brief moment in the interval when the eyes of both were turned away from the entrance they were placed to guard, seemed to calculate upon passing them unobserved. It was an exceedingly delicate manœuvre, and required great care and dexterity to effect it; but, at last, it was adroitly done, and the stranger sprang lightly through the entrance, secreting himself behind one of the pillars in the inner court of the palace. The sentinels paced on undisturbed.

"The figure which had thus stealthily effected an entrance, now sought the broad stairs that led to the governor's suite of apartments, with a confidence that evinced a perfect knowledge of the place. A second guard-post was to be passed at the head of the stairs; but, assuming an air of authority, the stranger offered a cold military salute and pressed forward, as though there was not the most distant question of his right so to do; and thus avoiding all suspicion in the guard's mind, he boldly entered the governor's reception-room unchallenged, and closed the door behind him. In a large easy chair sat the commander-in-chief, busily engaged in writing, but alone. An expression of undisguised satisfaction passed across the weather-beaten countenance of the new-comer at this state of affairs, as he coolly laid aside his cloak and proceeded to wipe the perspiration from his face. The governor, looking up with surprise, fixed his keen eyes upon the intruder.

"'Who enters here, unannounced, at this hour?' he asked, sternly, while he regarded the stranger earnestly.

"'One who has information of value for the governor-general. You are Tacon, I suppose?'

"'I am. What would you with me? or, rather, how did you pass my guard unchallenged?'

"'Of that anon. Excellency, you have offered a reward for information concerning the rovers of the gulf?'

"'Ha! yes. What of them?' said Tacon with undisguised interest.

"'Excellency, I must speak with caution,' continued the new comer; 'otherwise I may condemn and sacrifice myself.'

"'You have naught to fear on that head. The offer of reward for evidence against the scapegraces also vouchsafes a pardon to the informant. You may speak on, without fear for yourself, even though you may be one of the very confederation itself.'

"'You offer a reward, also, in addition for the discovery of Marti—Captain Marti, of the smugglers—do you not?'

"'We do, and will gladly make good the promise of reward for any information upon the subject,' replied Tacon.

"'First, Excellency, do you give me your knightly word that you will grant a free pardon to *me*, if I reveal all that you require to know, even embracing the most secret hiding-places of the rovers?'

"'I pledge you my word of honor,' said the commander.

"'No matter how heinous in the sight of the law my offences may have been, still you will pardon me, under the king's seal?'

"'I will, if you will reveal truly and to any good purpose,' answered Tacon, weighing in his mind the object of all this precaution.

"'Even if I were a leader among the rovers myself?'

"The governor hesitated for a moment, canvassing

in a single glance the subject before him, and then said :

"'Even then, be you whom you may; if you are able, and will honestly pilot our ships and reveal the secrets of Marti and his followers, you shall be rewarded as our proffer sets forth, and yourself receive a free pardon.'

"'Excellency, I think I know your character well enough to trust you, else I would not have ventured here.'

"'Speak, then; my time is precious,' was the impatient reply of Tacon.

"'Then, Excellency, the man for whom you have offered the largest reward, dead or alive, is now before you!'

"'And you are——'

"'Marti!'

"The governor-general drew back in astonishment, and cast his eyes towards a brace of pistols that lay within his reach; but it was only for a single moment, when he again assumed entire self-control, and said,—

"'I shall keep my promise, sir, provided you are faithful, though the laws call loudly for your punishment; and even now you are in my power. To insure your faithfulness, you must remain at present under guard.'

"Saying which, he rang a silver bell by his side, and issued a verbal order to the attendant who answered it. Immediately after, the officer of the watch entered, and Marti was placed in confinement, with orders to render him comfortable until he was sent for. His name remained a secret with the commander: and thus the night scene closed.

"On the following day, one of the men-of-war that lay idly beneath the guns of Moro Castle, suddenly became the scene of the utmost activity, and, before noon, had weighed her anchor, and was standing out into the Gulf Stream. Marti, the smuggler, was on board, as her pilot: and faithfully did he guide the ship, in the discharge of his treacherous business, among the shoals and bays of the coast for nearly a month, revealing every secret haunt of the rovers, exposing their most valuable depôts and well selected rendezvous; and many a smuggling craft was taken and destroyed. The amount of money and property thus secured was very great; and Marti returned with the ship to claim his reward from the governor-general, who, well satisfied with the manner in which the rascal had fulfilled his agreement, and betrayed those comrades who were too faithful to be tempted to treachery themselves, summoned Marti before him.

"'As you have faithfully performed your part of our agreement,' said the governor-general, 'I am now prepared to comply with the articles on my part. In this package you will find a free and unconditional pardon for all your offences against the laws. And here is an order on the treasury for ——'

"'Excuse me, Excellency. The pardon I gladly receive. As to the sum of money you propose to give me, let me make you a proposition. Retain the money, and in place of it, guarantee me the right to fish in the neighborhood of the city, and declare the trade in fish contraband to all except my agents. This will richly repay me, and I will erect a public market of stone at my own expense, which shall be an ornament to the city, and which at the expiration of a specified number of years shall revert to the government, with all right and title to the fishery.'

"Tacon was pleased at the idea of a superb fish-market, which should eventually revert to the government, and also at the idea of saving the large sum of money covered by the promised reward. The singular proposition of the smuggler was duly considered, and acceded to; and Marti was declared in legal form to possess for the future, sole right to fish in the neighborhood of the city, or to sell the article in any form; and he at once assumed the rights that the order guaranteed to him. Having in his roving life learned all the best fishing-grounds, he furnished the city bountifully with the article, and reaped yearly an immense profit, until, at the close of the period for which the monopoly was granted, he was the richest man on the island. According to the agreement, the fine market and its privileges reverted to the government at the time specified, and the monopoly has ever since been rigorously enforced."

Many romantic stories are told of Marti; but the one just related is the only one, I believe, that is authenticated, and which has any connexion with this monopoly.

To-morrow I expect to leave for Matanzas, Cardenas, and other places in the interior of the island. If I see anything of the "Cuban elephant" during my absence, I shall endeavor to photograph his "Imperial Majesty," and will transmit you a copy immediately on my return to this city.

LETTER IX.

HAVANA, *March*, 1856.

DURING my recent excursion into the country, I discovered many new and attractive features in Cuban life and scenery, of which I shall ever retain a pleasing remembrance. At the same time, I was a participator in a few "stirring scenes," and adventures of a less agreeable nature. I was accompanied as far as Guines—a small village lying on the railroad about fifteen leagues from the city—by a party of friends on their way to an *ingénio* (pronounced inhanyo) or sugar manufactory, situated a few miles from that station.

The cars on this road are of American manufacture (that is, built in the United States), are drawn by American-built engines, and conducted by American engineers. They are divided into three classes.

The rate of fare in each corresponds with the luxury of the accommodations. The first class are like the ordinary coaches on our northern railroads, but the fare in them is so high, that they are seldom patronized except by foreigners and wealthy planters when accompanied by ladies. The second class cars have seats without cushions; a covering overhead, but no protection at the sides or ends, which are open to the winds of heaven, blow they ever so roughly. But as the weather here is never cold, and storms are of rare occurrence, these cars are generally well filled, as the expense is much less, and the occupants are better able to see the country through which they are passing. The cars of the third class are simply uncovered platforms, for the transportation of slaves, coolies, and the lower order of the peasantry.

We reached Guines about nine o'clock A. M., and while breakfast was being prepared for our party, Mr. S—— and myself called on the wife of the *ventero* to show us the rooms that we could occupy on our return from the plantation that night. Being busy at the time with her matutinal preparations, our dark-skinned hostess deputed an unwashed and unkempt specimen of humanity—apparently of the male gender—to wait on us. We followed our guide through a large back-yard, swarming with pigs and poultry, to a dingy out-building, which contained two or three rooms, separated from each other by rough board partitions. These apartments were so dirty and uncomfortable, that we decided *not* to engage them; which decision was strengthened by the discovery that there were no inside fastenings to any of the doors, and no way to prevent the intrusion of the "outside barbarians," were any of them disposed to pay us a nocturnal visit. On our way back to the inn I noticed two suspicious-looking fellows seated on the ground playing at *monté*, a favorite game of cards with the peasantry. This discovery so affected the sensitive organization of my friend the Ex-Congressman, that he expressed a determination to return to Havana that night, being satisfied with his limited acquaintance with Cuban society and scenery.

The untidy appearance of the place, both in and out of doors, had such an *un*appetizing effect upon us, that we did not wait for breakfast, but left immediately for the *ingénio;* Mr. and Mrs. S—— in an old rickety volante, and I on an old and apparently rickety horse, whose powers of locomotion, however, proved to be much superior to what I was led to expect from his dilapidated appearance. If you have any conception of the shape of "a Virginia rail-fence," you can perhaps form some idea of the road over which we travelled. It was tortuous in the extreme, and its boundaries not being defined by fence or hedge, the postillion and guide was at liberty to select his way *ad libitum*. Soon after we started, my steed, either disliking the spur affixed to my heel or not understanding my Yankee dialect, increased his speed to such a degree that I was obliged to let go the small cord substituted for reins, and cling with tenacity to the saddle. After a ride of half a mile or so, John-Gilpin-like, my impetuous charger halted at a rustic cabin, where he evidently had, at some former time, been *horse*-pitably entertained. I there made some alterations in the bridle, and keeping my heels (particularly the offending one) as far from his susceptible sides as possible, succeeded in reaching my place of destination in safety.

After waiting two or three hours without seeing or

5*

hearing anything from the rest of our party, some six or eight in number, my friends made a hasty examination of the premises and returned to Guines, leaving me to pursue the rest of my journey alone. I subsequently learned that Mr. and Mrs. S—— having unknowingly taken the only public volante in that enterprising town, no conveyance could be procured for the other ladies, consequently they all took the return train to Havana without having accomplished the object of their journey.

I remained at this *ingénio* long enough to give it a careful examination, and to obtain from the gentlemanly proprietor much valuable information. This estate contains two thousand acres, nearly three-fourths of which are now planted with cane, which produces, on an average, about fifteen hundred hogsheads of sugar each year, besides a small quantity of molasses, and a liquor called *aguardiente*, a kind of domestic rum made from the refuse cane. These cane fields, in the distance, look like immense fields of giant broomcorn; with nothing to break the monotony, except the white mansion of the overseer, surrounded by a few straggling shade-trees, and the large sugar manufactory, with dense volumes of black smoke ascending from its tall, spectre-like chimney.

The cane ripens but once a year, and must be cut as soon as it is sufficiently mature. Therefore, during the cutting season all the available help on the plantation is brought into requisition—old and young, male and female; in fact, every creature that is strong enough to wield a *machéte*, or cutting knife, is obliged to labor in the field during the entire day and a part of the night, until the cane is cut and secured. In the sugar districts of the United States, the cane has often to be cut and manufactured within a period of four or five weeks, to escape the frost, and frequently has to be gathered before it is fully ripe. But here, the season is always favorable for ripening the cane, which grows almost spontaneously. Little or no labor is necessary in its cultivation, and the time for gathering the cane and making it into sugar, is extended through a period of from three to four months. In Louisiana the cane has to be replanted nearly every year. But the climate here is so favorable, and the soil so deep and fertile, that it will produce satisfactory crops for eight or ten years without being renewed; and there are estates on this island that have not been replanted within the memory of the oldest inhabitants. It is said that the cane-fields on the island of St. Thomas, which were planted more than a century ago by the Portuguese, still flourish and yield remunerating crops. These facts show the great disadvantages under which sugar planters in the Southern States labor, compared with those similarly engaged in Cuba and other tropical countries.

There are two methods of making sugar on this island. One is called the "centrifugal process," where steam and machinery are employed: the other the "claying process," where the work is chiefly done by manual and animal labor. The first is very expeditious, but requires complicated machinery, skilful engineers, and a large outlay of capital. The other is more simple and less expensive, but requires a much longer time in its manufacture. This *ingénio* is conducted upon the first-named plan, and the manner of making sugar here is substantially as follows. After the cane is cut and the green top removed, the main stalk is carried to the crushing-mill and the juice pressed out between two immense cylindrical rollers moved by steam. The crushed cane is then taken away by the women and children and spread out in the sun, like new-mown hay, to dry. When sufficiently cured it is housed in sheds, erected for the purpose, to be used as fuel for the engines. The cane-juice passes from the crushing-mill directly into an immense reservoir beneath; from there it is conducted into shallow vats filled with small steam pipes, which purge the juice from all extraneous matter. It is next transferred to a long row of copper caldrons, where it is boiled down to a sirup, the scum being removed as fast as it appears on the surface. After it has attained the requisite color and consistency, it is drawn off into large shallow vats to cool. By the side of these vats are arranged a number of circular iron hoppers each holding a bushel or more. These hoppers, or rather cylinders, are double thickness; the outside being of solid iron, while the lining is of fine wire cloth, with a space of a few inches between. This space is filled with the saccharine mixture, and the hopper which is connected with the engine is set in motion. After it has made several thousand revolutions, at the rate of about two thousand each minute, the motion is arrested and you discover that the inner surface of the wire cylinder is thickly covered with rich yellow sugar, beautifully crystallized and ready for use. What falls to the bottom is molasses, which is put up in hogsheads for market, or used for distillation. The sugar made by this "centrifugal process," called "Muscovado," is about the only kind sent to the United States for refining and other purposes. The other process is slow and tedious compared with that just described, although the clayed sugar is whiter, and in some respects superior in quality to the muscovado. After the juice is boiled down to the required consistency, it is put into tin or earthen moulds shaped like a funnel, each holding about fifty pounds. On the top is placed a layer of soft pipe-clay an inch or two in thickness, the liquid portion of which percolates through the sugar and carries all impurities with it out at the orifice. In three or four weeks the dry clay is removed from the top, the funnel inverted, and a large cone of sugar is presented to the view. It is usually divided into three qualities: that portion of the loaf through which the clay first passes being the purest, is put up in boxes by itself, and is known to the commercial world as white Havana sugar. This is the best quality to be obtained here, and is about equal to our lowest grades of white coffee-sugar.

The manual labor on these plantations is performed almost entirely by slaves—" Congoes" as they are called here, and " Coolies" from the Celestial Empire. These two classes of operatives, though intimately associated, are by no means alike in appearance or disposition. The former are natives of Africa, jet black, with short crispy hair, and are slaves *for life*. The latter are of Asiatic origin, copper-colored, with long, straight, black hair, and are slaves for a *term of years*. They are less stubborn and intractable than the negro, but more crafty, unprincipled, and revengeful; and if thwarted in any of their designs, or punished, however slightly, for any offence, they frequently commit suicide, knowing that the loss of their services would be a serious inconvenience, if not a great pecuniary misfortune to their masters. It appears that these Coolies go into servitude voluntarily. They enter into contract with the importer or his agent in China, to serve them or their assigns during a term of eight years from the date of the agreement, for the nominal sum of four dollars a month. At the expiration of that time they are to be sent back to their own country—if they are alive and desire to return—free of charge or expense to themselves. A bond to that effect is required by the Chinese authorities before they will allow their subjects to be taken away. So great is the demand on this island for the labor of these orientals, that the importer frequently receives a bonus of three or four hundred dollars per head for their services during eight years, notwithstanding their ignorance of the Spanish language, liability to disease, and well-known propensity to commit suicide upon the slightest provocation. Cargoes of these oriental productions are of frequent arrival, and their importation has become an important item in the commerce of Cuba.

During the manufacturing season—a period of about four months—the *ingénio* presents a scene of unceasing labor and activity. The engine is kept at work night and day, and the slaves are allowed but four or five hours' sleep out of the twenty-four; although at other times they can, if they choose, sleep from the setting to the rising of the sun. Notwithstanding this increase of labor, the slaves do not appear to dread the sugar season, for they are better fed during that period, and are allowed many privileges and indulgences that they do not have at other times, and which, to them, are more than equivalent to any excess of labor that may be imposed on them.

The growing of cane is very profitable. It affords a much larger profit on the outlay than either coffee or tobacco; consequently the cultivation of the latter products has been considerably neglected here of late. Some of the largest and best managed *ingénios* on this island yield an income of over two hundred thousand dollars, while the profits of many of the smaller estates average from fifty to a hundred thousand annually. Some of these wealthy planters being ambitious to improve the pedigree of their posterity, as well as their own social position, purchase for themselves a title from the court of Spain, that of a *cónde* or count costing about twenty-five thousand dollars. This class are designated as "sugar noblemen," and are looked upon with extreme disfavor by the old Spanish noblesse, most of whom inherit their titles from their ancestors. They regard these new-fledged aristocrats of plebeian origin as impertinent interlopers, and unfit associates for the genuine Castilian nobility or their lineal descendants.

Society here appears to be divided into three or four distinct classes or grades. First in point of caste—according to the Spanish classification—are the natives of old Spain, comprising many of the nobility, the clergy, officers in the army and under government, and a few planters and merchants. Class number two comprises the lawyers, bankers, merchants, planters, and retired citizens of wealth among the creoles or native Cubans. In this class are also to be found many persons of wealth, intelligence, and with sufficient capacity to "scale the highest round in ambition's ladder," were there not insuperable barriers to their progress in that direction. According to the Spanish laws, no native Cuban can hold any office of honor, trust, or emolument on this island, either in the army, the church, or under government. They are not even allowed to serve as privates in the regular army, although a regiment of free blacks is now in the volunteer service. The rigid exclusion from all offices of honor and trust in the land of their birth is extremely galling to the creole population, many of whom regard with an uncompromising dislike those sent here from the mother country to rule over them, and to be supported at their expense. This is literally the case; for Cuba pays all the expenses of its own government, both civic and military; maintains a standing army of at least thirty thousand soldiers, besides an inconsiderable navy; supports a great number of priests and clergy, and sends an annual remittance to Spain. The third class is composed of free negroes (of which there are about one hundred and fifty thousand on the island), half-breeds, and the lowest order of the peasantry. The fourth class comprises the coolies and the entire slave population, "numbering not far from five hundred thousand *souls;*" but this phrase is a solecism, as the Cubans do not generally allow that their slaves have any *souls* except those supplied by nature to their pedal extremities.

The laws of Cuba in regard to slavery are so stringent and rigidly enforced that the slaves on this island are exempt from many of the abuses they receive in the Southern States, although there is apparently no affection existing between master and slave. According to the Cuban slave code, those only between the ages of sixteen and sixty can be tasked, and when incapacitated for labor they are to be allowed a permanent subsistence.

They are not to be worked more than ten hours a day except during the sugar season, when they may be employed for sixteen or eighteen hours, but with an increased quantity of food, including a few specified luxuries. The quantity of food, both animal and vegetable, for their daily allowance, and the clothing they are to have during the year, is regulated by law. On Sundays and during the Holy days, they are not to be employed more than two hours in the service of their masters, except when the gathering of the sugar-cane admits of no delay; the rest of the time they must be allowed to attend to their gardens and private occupations. They are also protected in the enjoyment of a certain amount of property, and may apply their earnings to the purchase of their liberty. Many have already availed themselves of this law, so favorable to emancipation, and it is supposed that there are at this time over a hundred thousand free-blacks on this island. The laws here are very stringent in regard to corporal punishment. No slave can receive more than twenty-five lashes for any offence; if he has committed a crime the judicial authorities must decide his mode of punishment, and as to its severity. A master who violates the slave-code is heavily fined, and sometimes punished by imprisonment.

After having "sugared up" my truculent steed with a generous allowance of cane (for quadruped as well as biped appears to be fond of the saccharine plant), and refreshed myself with a few of the delicious products of the orange tree, I rode over to a *cafetal*, or coffee plantation, some two miles distant, where I spent an hour or two very pleasantly. This estate was not in a very prosperous condition, and did not quite come up to my expectations. I had heard such glowing descriptions of these plantations, that I expected to witness a scene of unsurpassed natural beauty; to revel amid such wealth of fruit, foliage, and flowers, that I would almost imagine myself in a terrestrial paradise. But I can easily imagine that a well arranged *cafetal* in full bloom and in a flourishing condition must be a beautiful sight. The coffee shrub attains a height of ten or twelve feet, but is usually kept "headed down" to about six feet, to facilitate the picking of the berries. It has large glossy leaves of a deep green color, and a profusion of white flowers which grow in clusters at the base of the leaf. It is generally planted in squares of about eight acres, separated from each other by broad avenues lined with double rows of cocoa-nut trees or palms. Extending over these squares, at regular intervals, are rows of banana, orange, lime, pomegranate, and other trees of smaller size and denser foliage, to protect the coffee-plant from the sun, its scorching rays being too severe for the delicate leaves and flowers. This plant is said to blossom five or six times during the year, although but a small portion of the flowers produce berries, which are at first green, then red, and when fully ripe of a deep brown color. It is seldom that more than two crops of coffee mature during the year, and the labor of tending, picking, drying, and shelling the berry, is performed by the slave women and children. To bring a coffee plantation into full bearing requires about four years. Each plant yields from eight ounces to a pound of coffee at a picking, and will continue to bear, if properly attended to, for a great number of years. This plant is not indigenous to Cuba, although the soil and climate are tolerably well adapted to its growth. The disastrous hurricanes which occasionally visit this island, damaging and destroying many of the coffee estates, together with its almost profitless culture, when compared with sugar, or even tobacco, have materially diminished its cultivation.

Notwithstanding the somewhat dilapidated appearance of this *cafetal*, it contained much that to me was novel and interesting; and I could imagine that in its prosperous days — when the innumerable trees which dot its squares were bending beneath the weight of their golden fruitage, and the various climbing plants, which now revel on tree-top and hedge, were covered with flowers of almost every hue and odor, and the coffee-shrub in full bloom, with its rich evergreen foliage profusely covered with snow-white flowers — it must indeed have been a beautiful sight, and pleasurably suggestive of the spot where our "first parents" passed the honey-moon.

The principal avenue leading from the highway to the house belonging to the estate was nearly a quarter of a mile long, and lined on each side with magnificent specimens of the royal palm—the *palma real* of Cuban fame, which is the monarch of all tropical trees as emphatically as the lion is king of all beasts. These palms were from fifty to sixty feet high. Their white, ring-circled bodies gently swelling in the centre and diminishing in circumference at each end, were of uniform size, and as perfect in shape as if fashioned by the plastic hand of man; without a limb, knot, or excrescence of any kind to mar the symmetry of their smooth and beautifully rounded bodies. The leaves were from ten to twenty feet long, a dozen or more forming the tuft or head of each tree, looking in the distance like immense plumes of ostrich-feathers. These grand old specimens of Cuban arborescence were planted on each side of the avenue at regular intervals, their drooping tops forming noble arches of living verdure, through which the golden sunlight faintly streamed, illuminating the "green solemnity" of this majestic colonnade.

This is unquestionably one of the richest botanical regions of the globe, and I have been very much interested in many of its wonderful productions. Not being familiar with the Spanish language, or skilled in the nomenclature of tropical trees and plants, I had considerable difficulty in finding out the names and habits of many of the trees peculiar to this island. It was truly a "pursuit of knowledge under difficulties," and if the description I shall here give of a few of the principal varieties be correct, I shall be satisfied that my well-meant labors have not been in vain.

The various kinds of palms are probably unsurpassed, for beauty and utility, by any of the large trees on this island. The wood is used for many kinds of building purposes, and the enormous leaves, when mature, for thatching the cottages of the natives; while the young foliage, when boiled, is said to be as delicate as cabbage, and its seeds or nuts are excellent food for swine. Each tree has about twenty leaves, which are shed at regular intervals during the year, leaving a circle of gum on the trunk, which remains indelible, and by that means the age of the tree can be determined with considerable certainty. The palm is said to live for more than two hundred years, and begins to bear fruit when about eighteen years old.

Among the trees most valued for its wood are the mahogany and the *Cedrela odoráta*, a species of cedar, which is available for a great variety of uses; cigar-boxes are made of it, also the doors of many dwellings, as it is susceptible of a polish almost equal to mahogany. Among the numerous other trees to which my attention has been directed, are the huge, ill-shaped ceyba, with its innumerable progeny of air-plants, which cover its branches, and enjoy a kind of "squatter sovereignty" on premises not their own; the lofty, cloud-aspiring cocoa-palm, with its green, tufted head depending in graceful beauty, and displaying its clusters of fruit at various stages of maturity, from the half-opened flower to the full-grown fruit; the indispensable calabash or " poor-man's furnishing-house," with its immense globular fruit of adamantine hardness, which supplies the natives with most of their culinary utensils; the tamarind, with its acidulous fruit, and delicately cut leaves of green, in beautiful contrast with the deep blue of the sky, as seen through its gossamer foliage; the bright and delicate bamboo, growing in luxuriant clumps, graceful in its form, and bending to the slightest breeze; and the mango, with its long racemes of kidneyshaped fruit, and with foliage so dense as to yield a grateful shade from the scorching rays of a tropical sun. Time will not permit me to describe all the fruit

> "The trees of this fair island bore,
> Whose balmy fragrance lured the tongue to taste
> Their flavors: Here bananas flung to waste
> Their golden flagons with thick honey filled!
> From splintered cups the ripe pomegranates spilled
> A shower of rubies: oranges that glow
> Like globes of fire, inclose a heart of snow!
> Here dates of agate and of jasper lay,
> Dropped from the bounty of the pregnant palm,
> And all ambrosial trees, all fruits of balm,
> All flowers of precious odors, made the day
> As sweet as a morn of paradise."

I was further reminded of the Garden of Eden, by

being shown a tree which some of the credulous natives believe to be the "Tree of Knowledge," which bore that fruit

————" whose mortal taste

Brought death into the world and all our woe."

This island abounds in parasitical plants, which creep over shrubs and trees, and like the hanging moss on the gums and cypresses of our southern forests, appear to derive most of their sustenance from the air. The *Jaquay-macho*, one of the most destructive of these parasites, commences to grow on the limbs or body of the tree; extending its fibres in every direction, and increasing in size and strength, until it wraps the whole tree in its fatal embrace. This death-struggle may continue for years, but in the end, this unfilial parasite, which nourishes itself with the life of its foster-parent, will be conqueror.

This phenomenon is thus explained. The seeds of the jaquay are carried by birds, or lodged by the wind among the branches of some neighboring tree, where they germinate, sending out numerous long slender fibres, which continue to grow until they reach the ground, where they take root. These fibres continue to multiply and increase in size until they cover the entire body of the tree, when they unite, forming a tree of themselves, the heart of which is the parent-tree, which first lent it support and gave it nourishment—a remarkable instance of filial ingratitude. It is said that when once the *jaquay* takes root, no tree, however large, can resist its destructive grasp. It winds itself around it with a slow, unyielding tenacity, and, like the insidious serpent, tightens its hold with every movement, however imperceptible, until it crushes or smothers its victim in its fatal embrace.

LETTER X.

HAVANA, *March*, 1856.

It was quite late in the afternoon when I set out on my return to Guines, in anticipation of spending a comfortless night at a miserable *venta* or inn, a place where they provide "entertainment for man and beast" on the same floor; and from what I saw in the morning, I judged that the sleeping-rooms were occupied by bipeds and quadrupeds alternately. I was a *stranger*, and expected to be "taken in," but *not* in the scriptural sense; was in the hands of the Philistines, but not having the strength of Samson, or any "jaw-bone" but my own to defend myself with, I knew not what was to be my fate.

While riding slowly along, absorbed in gloomy meditations, I was startled by the sound of voices as if in altercation. Looking up, I beheld a spectacle so ludicrous that my risibles were excited in an unusual degree. It was a *rustico*, or native peasant, returning from town, seated on the posteriors of a diminutive animal, with his *larger*-half in front of him. One arm was around her waist, while with the other he guided his Rosinante, which I imagined belonged to the "genus asinine," from the length of its ears, that being about the only part of the animal visible. The man was quietly smoking a cigar, while the woman—evidently a virago—was talking Spanish with wonderful volubility; and from her rapid gesticulations and excited manner, I judged that her conversation was not likely to become insipid from want of sufficient acrimony. This loving couple appeared much better able to carry the animal they rode, than the animal to carry them; but not being a reformer of abuses, like the chivalrous Knight of La Mancha, I did not think it best to remonstrate.

A little further on I met a mountain cavalier, on a spirited horse, with sword and pistols by his side, and with silver spurs so highly burnished, that they glittered in the bright sunlight like a cluster of diamonds. As he passed me, he very politely touched his sombrero, and with a "*buenos dias, Señor*" (good day, sir), was soon lost in the distance. These *monteros* inherit from their Moorish ancestors their peculiar attachment for the horse, and they are accustomed to the saddle from their early youth. A horse, sword, and silver spurs, generally comprise his estate—both real and personal. With these chattels he is as independent and happy as if the undisputed possessor of a well-stocked plantation. They are to *him* not only a luxury, but a positive necessity, and as indispensable to his maintaining "a position" in upper-tendom, as is a volante to the social elevation of a Cuban señorita. When I first discovered this armed horseman approaching on a full gallop, I confess I was a little startled, for we were a long distance from any habitation, and I had been told at the *ingénio* that a robbery had been committed in that vicinity the week before; but his respectful salutation relieved me at once from all unpleasant suspense. Spanish robbers have the reputation of being exceedingly polite, and many curious stories are told illustrative of their peculiar *suaviter in modo*. One that I heard recently, exhibits such a rare combination of Yankee assurance with true Chesterfieldian politeness, that I will relate it. A traveller on horseback was accosted, in an unfrequented part of the country, by a footpad. "Sir," said he to the gentleman, as he seized his horse by the bridle, "I see that you are riding my horse; let me assist you to dismount!" The traveller deliberately drew a pistol from his pocket, and pointing it at the fellow's head, asked him to look again and see if he were not mistaken. "Señor," said the highwayman, bowing very low as he relinquished his hold of the bridle, "I perceive my mistake. Please to honor me with your card, that I may remember you hereafter in my prayers!"

As I approached Guines the sky began to darken, and fearing a storm, I put spurs to my horse (notwithstanding my former mishap), and rode into town at an accelerated pace. As I entered the first street, a man rushed out of an adjacent building, seized my horse by the bridle, and thrusting his brawny hand into my face, vociferated "*quarto péso.*" My *first* thought was of robbery; but a second convinced me that the man was the owner of the animal I was on, and only intended to adopt the Cuban mode of robbery by *extortion*—a less summary, but equally vexatious mode of being relieved of one's money. I dismounted, and handed the fellow a quarter-eagle, which was more than he was legally entitled to, and more than I was directed to pay by the gentleman who procured the animal for me in the morning. He threw down the coin, and again vociferated "*quarto péso*" (four dollars). Not being able to speak *his* language intelligibly, nor he to understand *my* vernacular, I began to move in the direction of the inn, closely followed by my excited companion, talking loudly and rapidly gesticulating. As we were passing the door of about the only respectable-looking house in that vicinity, he seized me by the arm, and pushing open the door led me into a room where two persons were seated at a table. I began to try to make my grievances known in execrable Spanish, aided by an attempt at pantomime, supposing that I was in the presence of some ubiquitous Spanish officials, when one of the gentlemen addressed me in English. They proved to be New Yorkers, who were boarding at this house, and I was assured by them that I had offered the man more than was his just due; it being the custom of the inhabitants here to extort from strangers *ad libitum*. They then called the proprietor of the house, who sent the fellow adrift with what I had at first paid him. At the solicitation of these "good Samaritans," I remained there during the night; had a comfortable room, and what was a still greater luxury in Cuba, a clean bed. In the morning, after partaking of a passably good breakfast, and making my grateful acknowledgments to my newly-made friends—I " went on my way rejoicing."

I reached Matanzas by rail the same evening, and to my surprise was not called upon to show my permit at the station, although surrounded by the omnipresent police, and meeting soldiers at almost every step. I attributed this unlooked-for exemption from Spanish vigilance, to the fact that just before leaving Havana I went into a *sastraria*—or tailor-shop—to procure a change of summer clothing, and could find but one suit large enough and that was made for a Spanish officer, which the proprietor let me have on my paying him an extra *peso*. Apparelled in this suit of blue and white (a kind of military undress), and a broad-brimmed sombrero, with my beard and mustache trimmed in the latest Cuban style, and my complexion, naturally dark, deepened by recent exposure to a tropical sun, into a genuine "Spanish brown," I was enabled to pass very well for a native as long as I kept *my mouth shut*. This I did at times from prudential motives; although I must acknowledge, that, during my sojourn at Havana and other places on this island, I have, with a few exceptions, been treated with the utmost civility by the inhabitants.

On the cars I met an intelligent American, the overseer of a sugar estate in this vicinity, who directed me to the "Union Hotel" as the best in Matanzas; at the same time he gave me to understand that I would find very poor accommodations. I am surprised that a city of nearly thirty thousand inhabitants should contain no better place of entertainment than this miserable little *posada*, dignified by the title of "hotel." It was a low, unpainted wooden building, a story and a half high, and contained about a dozen miserable seven-by-nine lodging rooms. The one I occupied was on the second floor, and barely large

A Night with the Insects. 141

enough to accommodate the furniture, which consisted of a narrow cot-bedstead, a cedar table, and one rickety chair. I found no difficulty in standing erect in *one* part of the room, but as the ceiling descended at an angle with the roof, the other side would only admit of a stooping posture. The room was neither plastered nor ceiled, with no window in the side or end, but a small hole in the roof to let the air *out* and the musquitoes *in*.

Making a virtue of necessity I spent one night in this miserable abode, which was all that I could endure, being so annoyed by cockroaches and other insects (for Cuban insects, like Spanish flies, are very *irritating*) that I got but little sleep. I lay all night rolling and tumbling on my bed of unrest engaged in the delightful occupation of fighting sanguinary musquitoes, and in praying for Morpheus or daylight to come to my relief. In the morning I arose with the sun, and thrusting my head out of the hole in the roof, snuffed the breezes of heaven with the avidity of a convict just escaped from some loathsome dungeon. Finding that breakfast would not be ready until nine o'clock (some three hours later), I contented myself with a roll and a cup of coffee prepared for some early riser, and called for my bill, which was *only* two dollars and a half—a very moderate demand for one night's lodging (but not sleeping), and "a hasty cup" of a miserable muddy mixture called coffee. However, I paid the bill without comment, being glad to get away at almost any pecuniary sacrifice, as I was fearful that another night of such wholesale depletion would not leave blood enough in my system to "honor the *bills*" of any other mercenary musquitoes that I might encounter during my peregrinations. One more such depletory ordeal, I opine, would bankrupt me physically, and leave me without sufficient vitality to pay *any* debt, save the final "debt to nature." * * * Matanzas has a population of over twenty-five thousand, and is next in commercial importance to Havana, which place it somewhat resembles; although its streets are considerably wider, and it has less the appearance of a tropical city. It has its Plaza de Armas like Havana, also a cathedral, hospital, barracks, and other public buildings. Yet the city itself is dull and uninteresting when compared with its more opulent neighbor. The country lying around Matanzas is quite elevated, and some of the scenery is wild and beautifully picturesque. Not far distant is a crescent-shaped mountain called the Cumbre, the top of which is nearly three thousand feet above the sea. It is a favorite resort for strangers, as it is easy of access and affords a panoramic view that, for extent, variety, and beauty, is unsurpassed in the tropics. Matanzas lies on the sloping lands between the Cumbre and the sea, and is gradually creeping up the sides of the mountain, whose summit is crowned with pleasant villas and the residences of the wealthy planters who own estates in the valley. The view from the top is almost boundless, extending at least fifty miles in several different directions. On one side was the city with its quaint old Moorish towers and turreted battlements; its low, parti-colored buildings, with flat tiled roofs, and its spacious harbor, in which many "a ship with folded wings lay sleeping on the tide." Beyond, was the broad, unfathomable ocean, with its myriads of white-capped waves—

"Chanting in wildly measured chorus
  Their hymn of majesty."

On the other side, at its very feet, as it were, reposed in quiet beauty the lovely valley of the Yumuri, with its waving fields of giant-cane, its cafetals and orange plantations, surrounded by hedges, and the white-winged mansions of the owners, half hidden in tropical verdure; with here and there a palm-thatched cottage with a solitary cocoa-nut tree, rising high above the roof, and overshadowing it like a protecting deity.

Scattered over the intervening space were groves of the mango, banana, orange, and other tropical fruits, with an occasional thicket of bamboo, their tall, green, waving, feathery forms, yielding to the slightest breeze, and glistening with an almost emerald brilliancy in the sunshine of a bright spring morning. It was a scene that cannot well be described; a picture that would require the magic pencil of a Titian to delineate.

On my return to the city, I repaired to the cathedral, where I witnessed a scene entirely different from the one I had just been contemplating. Here was a display of priests and pageantry, of incense and adoration. Here were beautiful ladies in rich attire, reclining upon gay bits of carpet spread on the marble floor. Here were spruce-looking señors in black dress-coats and white gloves, bowing before the altar, but evidently more interested in their fair fellow-worshippers than in the prosy pater-nosters of the portly bishops and sanctimonious priests. The interior of the church was profusely decorated with gold and silver ornaments and artificial flowers. The gilded trappings of the various altars glistened in the light of innumerable wax candles, and the air was fragrant with incense from censers borne about by young novitiates, in embroidered caps and sacerdotal robes. These, together with the festal costumes of the audience, who were constantly coming and going, presented rather an undevout aspect to a stranger and a Protestant.

A company of soldiers soon came marching in to the sound of the fife and drum. Stacking their arms in the centre of the church, they dropped on one knee, and with bowed heads and arms crossed upon their breasts awaited their turn at the confessional, which was then occupied by the "less sinful sex." I judged, however, from the length of time some of them were engaged with their confessors, that their sins must have been very *scarlet*. I observed that the youngest and best looking priests were assigned to the ladies. This might have been accidental, but I could not help thinking that it was so designed. These padres sat in their confessional boxes, with their faces close to the lattice-work separating them from the fair kneeling penitents, who were listening to the words of consolation or—something else—which Dame Rumor says these wily priests not unfrequently delight to pour into their *two* willing ears. The Cuban ladies have the reputation of being particularly susceptible to the tender passion, and oft-times " love not wisely, but too well."

I have been very much impressed here, as well as in Havana, with the disparity in size and physical development between the Cuban ladies and gentlemen of the better classes. The gentlemen, as a sex, are the most diminutive specimens of male humanity that I have ever seen. I refer more particularly to the Cuban aristocracy, for the *highest* classes, to speak paradoxically, are perpendicularly the *lowest*. The cause of this diminution in stature has been attributed to excessive smoking during their boyhood, and intermarriage of kindred during many generations. The men are as remarkable for tenuity as the women for plumpness. The males are small, thin—mere atomic specimens of humanity, while the females are almost without exception rotund, and of fair proportions. Notwithstanding the Cuban ladies, both plebeian and patrician, are slightly *embonpoint*, they are instinctively graceful and easy in their bearing. They have not the elastic step and Terpsichorean agility of the French; but "a seducing grace of motion," an impassioned *abandon* of manner, characterize all their movements, whether at worship in church, coquetting on the Plaza, or in the giddy mazes of the dance, when

> "to the low voluptuous swoons
> Of music, rise and fall the moons
> Of their full brown bosoms."

How gracefully they float through the delicious mazes of the *contradanza*, to the soft entrancing music of that luxurious dance! Their graceful motions and undulating movements are but the "rhythmic utterances" of their most-too-tropically-languid lives. The *contra-*

danza is the dance, par excellence, of the Cuban *salons;* while the *fandango,* accompanied by the tinkling of a guitar and the lively rattle of the inspiring castanets, is the favorite with the peasantry. They dance upon the lea, by the wayside, or beneath the shade of some umbrageous tree or vine-clad bower. In fact, whenever a few of these rustic belles and beaux meet together after the labors of the day, if a guitar can be had, they are sure to indulge in their favorite amusement. These peasant women dance well from instinct, and in all their movements they exhibit a peculiar grace, with a freedom from those awkward gestures and unbecoming attitudes so often to be seen among that class of females in the United States. A recent traveller in Cuba has expressed his belief that a really awkward woman does not exist on the island. Whether bred in the city or country, in the humble cottage of the montero, in the retired mansion of the planter, or the lowly dwelling of the artisan, she is sure to be easy and graceful in her bearing, if not possessed of all the polish and dilettanteism of an educated and highly cultivated life.

My next stopping-place was Cardenas, a flourishing

sea-port town of some six thousand inhabitants, the great Cuban mart for sugar and molasses. Thousands of hogsheads were piled upon its wharves, ready for shipment, and its numerous warehouses were literally "running over" with treacle. As there was but little to interest me in and around Cardenas, my stay there was short. The evening of the second day found me on board of a small steamer which plies between that place and Havana. Not being familiar with the rules and regulations of Cuban steamboats, or acquainted with the language, I was at a loss how to procure a stateroom or berth for the night. During my school-boy days I was often made to "walk Spanish," but was never taught the dialect; consequently, I could not obtain the information I desired in a legitimate way, and was obliged to substitute Yankee assurance for Spanish cognition, and abide the result.

Among the passengers who came on board, I noticed a stout, thick-set, benevolent-looking individual, who attracted my attention from his being the most adipose specimen of male humanity that I had seen during my stay on the island. He was well-dressed, scrupulously neat in his appearance, and carried a cigar behind his ear, in the place of a pen, giving to him a commercial air, and establishing beyond peradventure his calling. I resolved in my mind to follow this man, and to imitate his movements as far as practicable. He proceeded immediately to the cabin, and placed the satchel he carried in his hand in an unoccupied berth. I did the same, then followed him to the ticket office, where he laid down a gold coin with the words "*boletin por Habana.*" I echoed his expression, tendered my coin, and the same results followed. I was quite elated at the success of my ruse, by which I had secured a passage-ticket and a berth for the night without the assistance of an interpreter, and added a few words to my vocabulary of Spanish without the aid of a text book, or any superfluous waste of the "midnight oil." Being in a peculiarly self-complacent mood, and not anticipating any further impediment to a successful voyage, I left the crowded passages of the vessel, and sought a retired place on deck where I could commune with Nature and my own thoughts undisturbed, and free from the annoyance of the combined odor of garlic and cigar-smoke.

The night was beautiful; the sky serene, and the

air of such transparent purity and balminess, that the very breathing of it was to me a luxury and a delight. I remained for hours inhaling the delicious, health-giving atmosphere, and contemplating the scene before me, which was of unsurpassed beauty and grandeur. The sombre Ocean with her depths unknown lay in one vast "melancholy waste" before me. The throbbings of her gigantic heart were hushed as if by some magic spell, as our little steamer pursued its almost trackless way over her calm unruffled bosom, with the solemn sky above

> "Like a blue curtain hung,
> And studded with its bright star-gems
> As diamonds yet unstrung."

While low down in the heavens was visible in all its splendor, through the soft transparent darkness, that brilliant cluster of stars known as the Southern Cross, with its foot apparently almost resting on the earth. This beautiful constellation—this bright gem in "the dusky tiara of night," is invisible in our latitude, but is here revealed in all its beauty. At midnight the cross is said to stand erect, but as the night wears away it begins to decline, and gradually sinks until lost to sight beneath the horizon's verge.

When I retired to the cabin, I found it occupied by a motley assemblage of persons, consisting of priests, officers, tradesmen, and others whose exterior gave no evidence of their occupation; but, if I may be allowed the Yankee prerogative of "guessing," I should say that many of them were dealers in cigars, or excessive smokers, from the enormous quantity of "the weed" which they carried with them. The man of substance, whose shadow I had been personifying, was lazily reclining in his berth, smoking a cigar, and looked the very picture of contentment and good-nature; so much so, in fact, that I was half inclined to doubt his being a native of the island. Near him was seated an officer, a grave Castilian, who preserved a dignified demeanor, and neither spoke nor noticed those by whom he was surrounded. Among the passengers were several sallow-faced priests, whose *barber*-ously denuded heads were surmounted by small square caps of black silk. They were all attired in the sombre garb of their order, and were remarkably quiet and unobtrusive in their deportment.

The heat of the atmosphere, together with the fumes of tobacco with which the cabin was filled, began to produce a somnolent effect upon me; consequently I retired to my berth, and after arranging my musquito net about me, sought communion with the drowsy god Morpheus. I had but just fallen asleep when I was awakened by a heavy hand on my shoulder. Starting up, I beheld standing over me a fierce-looking Spaniard, with a Moorish complexion, which, by the dim light of a single lamp, looked black and defiant as a jealous Othello. He was talking loudly, and apparently much excited. I soon discovered that *I* was the innocent cause of this fierce ebullition of passion. I had evidently got into the wrong berth; the one I occupied was his by *berth*-right, but mine by possession. Finding that he could not make me understand his vernacular, he left the cabin, and in a few minutes returned with one of the officers of the vessel. They both tried by expressive pantomime and unintelligible Spanish, to make me sensible of my "poaching proclivities;" but in vain. I could not be made to understand,— was dull of comprehension,—as stupid as Balaam's ass, and would not be moved by the *jaw*-bone even of a voluble Spaniard. To their oft repeated harangues I shook my head and replied, "Me Americano, no Español," and at last impudently turned my back to them, drew the bed-clothes over my head, and feigned sleep. They remained near me for some time, talking in an excited manner, but at length their voices became less and less distinct, and finally died away in the distance.

I lay for awhile perfectly still, but at length removed the covering from my face, opened one eye, and cast an anxious glance at the foot of my berth to see if my clothes and satchel were safe, and then took a survey of the apartment. A number of men were seated at a table playing cards, two or three were dozing in their chairs, and one was stretched at full length on the floor, his head pillowed on a knapsack, and snoring loudly. My nervous system had received such a shock that I found it impossible to compose myself to sleep. I lay the remainder of the night in a half-unconscious state, between sleeping and waking, haunted by visions of gorgons, ogres, and other fabulous monsters. At daylight our steamer was safely

Return to Havana.

anchored in the harbor of Havana, and I was happy to be once more domiciled beneath the comparatively hospitable roof of the Revere Hotel, being satisfied with my somewhat limited acquaintance with Cuban society and scenery.

LETTER XI.

HAVANA, *March*, 1856.

I HAVE as yet said but little relative to the customs and domestic habits of the Cubans, who are a peculiar people. Though of more mercurial temperaments than their ancestors, the Moors and Spaniards, they inherit many of the characteristics of those nations. They have the reputation of being crafty, subtle, and intriguing in their natures, and exceedingly lax in their morals; yet, strange as it may appear, they are, with few exceptions, an orderly, law-obeying, priest-fearing, but not a God-serving people. Notwithstanding nearly every one goes armed, instances of assassinations or even encounters are less frequent than in our own country. And what was still more surprising to me, they are quite temperate both in eating and drinking. I have not observed a single instance of gross and manifest intoxication among the inhabitants during my stay on the island. Their principal beverage is a light, sour, native wine, somewhat resembling Catalonian wine. It is quite acid, but not inebriating in its effects, unless drunk in extravagant quantities.

The prevalent and all-absorbing vice in this country is gambling. This passion pervades all classes of society, from the noble count, with his broad acres and army of slaves, to the native peasant and humble artisan. The *Plaza de Toros,* where bull-fights are held, and the numerous cock-pits scattered over the island, are government property, from which the Crown of Spain derives no inconsiderable revenue. On Sundays and high festivals, cock-fighting and bull-fighting offer their chief attractions. In fact, I have been told that the law regulating these amusements forbids their taking place on any other days than Sundays and religious holidays. Monte is the popular game of cards with the Cuban peasantry, who spend many an idle hour stretched upon the ground beneath the shade of some favorite tree, engaged in this seductive amusement. When once they begin to play, they will not leave off as long as either has a *peséta* in his pocket, or a *camisa* on his back; and they frequently become so excited in the game as to stake their entire wardrobe on the result, leaving one of them at the close almost *in puris naturalibus*, that is to say, with but little more covering than was furnished him by Dame Nature when he was first ushered into this "breathing world." A few years ago gambling was practised here as openly and as undisguisedly as at many of the German watering-places. But I learn that an effort is being made by the authorities here to suppress all kinds of gambling, where no revenue will be lost to the government by their discontinuance. Notwithstanding this, the vice is prevalent, particularly on the Sabbath and during the Holy days, both of which might with propriety be termed holidays. For there is, in reality, no Sabbath here; no day of physical rest; no cessation from labor; no abatement of pleasures. From the rising of the sun to the setting of the same (except during midday), even to a late hour at night, it is one continued round of excitement, of gaieties, and amusements. The ringing of bells, firing of cannon, and the sound of martial music usher in the Sabbath morning. The various shops and stores are open as on all other days. The theatre, *mascaráda*, and Plaza de Toros, are made a *specialité* on that occasion; cries are heard in the streets from the venders of fruits and vegetables; and everything pertaining to business or pleasure assumes on that day a more than ordinarily busy aspect. How entirely unlike a Sabbath in any of our northern towns, and how at variance with the sentiments and feelings of one brought up to respect that holy day. And yet the inhabitants all seem to be impressed with no small degree of reverence for their priests and their religion. The peasant market-man, with his long line of heavily-laden mules, bows his head and makes the sign of the cross when he passes a church; the sable *calesero*, as he dashes by with his mistress in her volante, lifts his sombrero reverentially; and the dirty, half-clad native children are taught to cease from playing, and to refrain from all noise or merriment when they are within its sacred precincts.

The visitor in Havana is continually reminded of the ubiquity of Romanism, and its peculiar influence on the minds and morals of the people. The "carrying of the Host" through the streets is a spectacle of frequent occurrence, and cannot fail to inspire one, particularly at night, with feelings of solemnity. The tinkling of a small bell usually announces the approach of the Host, when every good Romanist within its sound uncovers his head, bends his knee, and maintains a devotional attitude until the procession has passed out of sight. These processions usually consist of half-a-dozen or more monks or friars, in long black robes (their closely shorn heads exposed without a cap or cowl), and a motley assemblage of men and boys bareheaded, and carrying in their hands long wax candles. In their midst is a priest bearing the consecrated symbol, to administer to some dying person. The number of lights displayed on these occasions, and the extent and magnificence of the retinue, are usually proportioned to the wealth and influence of the invalid or his family. Sometimes the priest who carries the sacred Host rides in a splendid coach drawn by four horses richly caparisoned and attended by outriders in livery, and military in full dress.

Last week was the closing of Lent, and during Holy Thursday and Good Friday a more than Protestant Sabbath-day stillness reigned throughout this entire city. The shops were all closed, the flags from the public buildings lowered, and during these two days not a volante or conveyance of any kind was allowed in the streets. The "carrying of the dead Christ," and the annual procession of the priests and military, took place during Good Friday afternoon and evening; and for several hours the various streets in the vicinity of the cathedral were thronged with pedestrians; and every balcony and house-top, as far as the eye could reach, was densely crowded with women and children waiting to see this pageant, which was evidently considered "the show of the season." A body of cavalry with prancing steeds and flashing sabres, prepared the way for the procession as it advanced. A martial band with muffled drums beating time to a funeral march, and a score or two of negroes in long black robes and immaculate turbans, and carrying blazing torches, led the way. Then came the archbishops, bishops, and high-priests in their canonical robes, followed by the "state bed" containing a wax figure representing "the dead Christ." Suspended above it was a gorgeously embroidered silken canopy, supported by four intensely rouged angels dressed in ethereal gauze, bespangled with imitation diamonds. This state bed was carried upon the heads of about a dozen men, whose feet alone were visible, their bodies being entirely hidden by the heavy folds of the voluminous drapery. Next in the procession was a retinue of priests, each carrying a long wax candle, or some emblem of the passion of Christ. In their midst were several richly decorated thrones containing the "Virgin Mother," "Mary Magdalene," and others, who were elaborately attired, and profusely covered with tinsel and artificial flowers. Then came a large body of civilians, in black dress-coats and white gloves, followed by several regiments of Spanish soldiers with their arms reversed and marching with slow and measured tread to the dirge-like music of their regimental bands. Last in the procession, but not least in point of numbers, were the unwashed multitude, of all colors and castes, who fell in the rear as an opportunity offered, adding greatly to the number, but not to the character of this great Easter demonstration.

The next day, the throne containing the Virgin Mary was borne with great pomp, parade, and ceremony, through the principal streets of the city, until it met the advancing procession with the image of the Saviour. As soon as Christ was found, a cannon was fired to apprise the inhabitants that fasting was at an end; flags appeared as if by magic, upon all the public buildings; bells were rung, guns fired, drums beaten, and every conceivable plan adopted to make a noise. Volantes appeared in the streets; negroes and creoles rushed wildly about, shouting and rejoicing; and a universal jubilee and jollification at once began.

The next evening I went with a party of American naval officers to the *Teatro de Tacon*, which was then open for the first time since the beginning of Lent. This celebrated theatre is on the Pasco Isabel, and nearly opposite the Monserrate gate, the principal entrance to the city. The exterior of the Tacon is not particularly attractive, but the interior is light, airy, well arranged for that climate, and very capacious, it being one of the largest theatres in America.

Here we witnessed a display of the ubiquitous soldiery. A company with glistening bayonets were stationed outside the door. Within, were jaunty little soldiers in white uniforms, who strutted about, shoving the creoles, and making way for gold-laced dignitaries; while officers in military undress were to be seen in all parts of the house, imparting to the audience a half-military and half-festive appearance.

If there were any "stars" in the dramatic horizon that evening, they were not, I opine, of the "first magnitude;" at least, they did not appear to dazzle the audience with their brilliancy, or to excite in them either mirthful or lachrymal emotions. For an interlude, we had an *animated* dissertation on the poetry of motion from one of the *corps de ballet*, which created quite a sensation among the appreciative portion of the audience, who were noisily demonstrative, as much to our annoyance as to the delight of the smiling *danzánta*, whom they assailed with bouquets, until the stage was almost covered with these floral evidences of their admiration.

I was very much surprised at the enthusiasm created by this votary of Terpsichore, for she was by no means a proficient in the saltatory art, neither was she young, or particularly attractive in person. Her eyes were not of a celestial blue, or like

> "The stars of a soft summer night,
> So darkly beautiful, so deeply bright."

Her teeth were not as Orient pearls, or her lips like two rosebuds growing on one stem. Her hair, though abundant, was not as glossy as the raven's plumage, or "as soft as the down that swells the cygnet's nest." Neither was hers

> "A pure, transparent, pale, and radiant face,
> Like to a lighted alabaster vase."

Her feet were not as delicate as a fairy's, or her form as symmetrical as a sylph's, but, like the sailor's wife at Wapping, she was "fat and forty," but not fair. She was rather above the medium height, with a well developed *physique*, and a decidedly gipsy countenance. Her hair was drawn back very unbecomingly behind her ears, displaying high cheek bones, and a complexion too ruddy to be beautiful. If hers was a "Spanish beauty," it did not by any means please our Anglo-Saxon fancy; and if she was an artist of much merit, we *Americanos* were too obtuse, or unskilled in "the divine art," to discover it.

The private boxes in this theatre are inclosed by light ornamental lattice-work, and it is customary for the audience, during the intermission, to wander through the cool passage-ways outside of the boxes, and to stop and gaze on the fair occupants within *à volonté*. Instead of being annoyed or displeased at this seemingly impertinent curiosity, the ladies are said to be rather gratified than otherwise at such attentions from strangers, which they construe into evidences of admiration.

I was not a little surprised to see, in one of the finest private boxes in the theatre, my landlady of the Revere. She was elegantly dressed, ornate with jewels, and attended by her cavalier, a gentleman I had frequently seen at the hotel, though ignorant of his name or occupation. I subsequently learned that it was Madame's ambition to occupy one of the most expensive and conspicuous boxes at the Tacon, and to excel in the splendor of her apparel her more opulent and aristocratic neighbors. Having sufficiently gratified our curiosity, we left the theatre before the performances were over. As I passed through the doorway, I unintentionally jostled a soldier on duty, who looked daggers at me in *Spanish;* but being in a hurry, I did not wait for an interpretation, presuming that it would not be very flattering to my vanity, or particularly euphonious to "ears polite."

At a *café* near by, where we discussed, over our chocolate and cigars, the evening's entertainment, we met a resident American acquaintance, who proposed taking us to a *Bal Masqué* not far distant. We gladly accepted his invitation, as none of our party had ever seen a Cuban *mascaráda*—that class of amusements having been discontinued during Lent. Under the guidance of our friend, who was familiar with the Spanish language and the "institutions" of this city, we repaired to the *Plaza de Máscaras*, or place of masks. Having procured our tickets at the door, we were admitted into a large but dimly-lighted room on the second floor, where about a hundred persons of both sexes were assembled. Many of the men had cigars in their mouths, and some smoked while dancing. A few of the other sex held small. cigarettes between their fingers, which they would occasionally place to their lips and puff out minute volumes of fragrant smoke. At one end of the room, on an elevated platform, were the musicians, with three or four stringed instruments, a horn, and a bass drum. The dancing had not commenced when we arrived, so that we had an opportunity to inspect the audience *in quiesco*. Most of the women were dressed, or rather half dressed (for their necks and shoulders were shockingly nude) in plain-colored barège or tarlatan, with a light mantle, of some dark material, to throw over them at pleasure. Some had their faces entirely concealed; but the youngest and evidently best-looking wore small silk vizors or demi-masks, hiding just enough of the face to give piquancy to the rest, and to create in the spectator a desire to see more. Those wearing dominoes, or fully masked, were supposed to be females of doubtful personal attractions, or whose position in society induced them to preserve a strict incognito; for it would be damaging to the reputation of any lady of respectability to be seen in such a place. Still, it is not probable that many go there who have any character or reputation to lose. A tolerably genteel appearance, and money enough to buy a ticket, are all that is necessary to obtain admission; consequently, men of all conditions in life, from the aristocratic *roué* to the humble mechanic and cigar-vender, patronize and participate in these midnight entertainments.

Soon after eleven o'clock the band began to tune their instruments, which was the signal for opening the ball. All was excitement among the Habaneros, who rushed here and there in pursuit of their partners, and as soon as possible secured a place on the floor. When all the available space was occupied, the music struck up, and the multitude rushed into the whirling vortex of the waltz with an *abandon* characteristic of a people who do nothing with moderation—not even the conducting of their religious worship and holy-day observances. The floor shook with the accumulated weight and motion of the numerous dancers, as they moved around the room, swaying to and fro in each other's embrace with a kind of delirious excitement, as if their senses were intoxicated with passion and delight;

"——— and when
Music arose with its voluptuous swell
Soft eyes look'd love to eyes that spoke again."

During a pause in the dancing, we mingled with the crowd, being desirous, during our brief stay here, to see as much as possible of this peculiar phase of Cuban life. It was evident that our party was creating quite a sensation among the audience, as there were several fine-looking officers in their showy uniforms, which usually attract the eyes of the ladies, at home and abroad. They were frowned upon by the jealous señors, but received many a sidelong glance and significant look from the fair señoritas, who, under pretence of arranging a stray lock of hair, or some similar device, would occasionally remove their masks sufficiently for us to see their faces. Several times during the evening, the Cuban ladies expressed to our Spanish-American acquaintance a desire to waltz with the "elegántes Americanos;" which honor was respectfully declined.

As it waxed far into the cigar-scented night, the mirth became more hilarious, and the dust from the sanded floor, with the smoke from innumerable cigars, imparted a sort of nebulous tinge to the atmosphere. It was almost a saturnalia; and the view from the background, through the dim perspective, was strangely suggestive of those gloomy mythological regions so graphically described by the old Latin poets. About half-past twelve we took our departure, having sufficiently gratified our curiosity, and added a few more items to our repertory of Cuban usages and customs. I was glad to get back to my comparatively quiet room at the Revere, being full to satiety of dust and tobacco-smoke, and weary of looking at beautiful human forms without human faces, and listening to

> "—— the lascivious tinklings
> Of lulling instruments, the softening voices
> Of women, and of beings less than women."
> * * * * * * * *

LETTER XII.

HAVANA, *April*, 1856.

THIS is my last night in Havana. To-morrow morning, Providence permitting, I shall bid adieu to this gem of the southern seas, beautiful Cuba. Her cane-covered fields; her vine-clad hills; her aromatic groves; her luscious fruits, I leave without regret; they are to me no longer "a feeling and a love." I have become weary with star-gazing and sight-seeing, surfeited with priests and pageantry, and disgusted with Spanish despotism and the odious aroma of garlic and cigar-smoke, which everywhere pervades the atmosphere of human habitations. I sigh once more for Columbia's happy land, with her free institutions and republican form of government, where liberty of speech and freedom of action are allowed; and I sincerely hope, if ever again I visit

Religious Intolerance.

this beautiful but ill-governed island, that some other flag more suggestive of freedom will wave from her hill-tops and towers.

Religious intolerance is a distinctive characteristic of this government. They are even less liberal here than in many parts of the mother country. Protestant worship is permitted in Madrid, but not here; neither are its doctrines—which are antagonistic to despotism—allowed to be disseminated on this island. The British and American consuls at Havana have applied for permission to hold religious worship in their houses on the Sabbath, without avail; and were it not for occasional services on foreign vessels in the harbor, visitors would have no opportunity to hear Protestant preaching.

I attended worship a few Sabbaths ago on board of a British man-of-war called the Powerful, which was anchored in the bay about a mile from the landing, and beyond the jurisdiction of popery. The commander, with true English politeness, sent his private barge for our party, and we were rowed to the vessel by six "jolly tars" dressed in their Sunday suits of immaculate blue and white. The "Powerful" is an eighty-four gun ship, with a complement of seven hundred and fifty men, including officers, marines, and sailors; all of whom, except those on duty, attended service, and were as quiet and orderly as any congregation I ever saw. The music was solemn, grand, and peculiarly impressive. A fine marine band was a substitute for an organ; while the clear tenor and rich soprano voices of the young boys of the naval school, harmonizing with the deep bass and diapason tones of those more advanced in years, combined to make a full and effective choir.

I was introduced by one of our party, an Episcopal clergyman of Boston, to the officiating chaplain, who very politely accompanied us about the ship, visiting the various apartments of this "Leviathan of the deep," which was almost a Sabbath-day's journey. We found ourselves very much fatigued from going down and up so many flights of stairs, and very gladly accepted our clerical friend's invitation to repair to his study and partake of refreshments, which we found already prepared. The time passed so pleasantly, that it was quite late in the day when we took our departure.

The next Sabbath I attended divine service on

board of the United States flag-ship Potomac, which is now here awaiting sailing orders from our government. The Rev. E. H. Renouf, from Boston, preached on the occasion, and gave us a plain, practical, orthodox sermon, without any affectation, or labored attempt at rhetorical display. He preached love to God and good-will to *all* men, dwelling especially on that greatest of all rarities, "Christian charity;" and his whole discourse was replete with such pure, unselfish, evangelical sentiments, as could not fail to meet the approval of all denominations. The services were similar to those on board of the British man-of-war, except that prayers were offered for the President of the United States, instead of her most gracious Majesty, Queen Victoria.

There are quite a number of American vessels now in this harbor, and the stars and stripes of our glorious republic float triumphantly in the breeze, and the American Eagle is emblazoned on the uniforms of scores whom I meet every day, imparting, as it were, a kind of energy and vitality to this land, scorched and dried up by the withering sirocco of Spanish misrule and papal despotism. * * * * * *

The next day, after the closing of Lent, a bull-fight was announced to take place in Havana in honor of the return of his Excellency General Concha, who had been absent from the city about a month. I resolved to attend, as it might be the only opportunity I would ever have to witness one of these exhibitions. But I will here say in extenuation—if any excuse or apology is necessary—that it was the most disgustingly brutal sight that I ever beheld, and nothing could ever induce me to witness a repetition.

The Plaza de Toros is situated nearly a mile beyond the walls of the city. Our party consisted of Dr. C. and young Mr. L. from the States, who were stopping at the Revere, and five or six of the officers belonging to the Potomac. We took volantes at the hotel, and soon found ourselves at the entrance to the grounds of the Plaza, in the midst of a motley crowd of Spaniards and natives, who were rushing towards the ticket-office shouting " Boléta," and holding in their extended hands the coin requisite for admission. Having procured our tickets in advance, we lost no time in elbowing our way to the door, where we found the rest of our party, who had preceded us.

Passing between a file of Spanish soldiers, we soon found ourselves within an extensive amphitheatre, around which were rows of covered seats rising one above the other, and capable of holding several thousand spectators. The arena for the exhibition was an open space of nearly half an acre; around the outside at regular intervals, were a number of strong wooden barriers, formed by heavy posts driven into the ground, behind which the combatants could take refuge when pursued by the infuriated bulls. The audience was large, comprising all grades, sexes, and colors—from the captain-general and his family, in their ornamented box, to the swarthy mule-driver from the mountains, who occupied with his dame or sweetheart a *standee* just outside the barriers. There were beautiful ladies richly attired and languishing beneath glittering diamonds and other personal decorations, and lovely children of the nobility, so very young as to be carried in the arms of their sable attendants.

The signal flag was hoisted, a trumpet blast heard, and the vast multitude were wild with excitement, as the various actors in the drama (or rather tragedy) entered the arena in a procession. First came the master of ceremonies, dressed in ancient Spanish costume, followed by six or eight *picadórs*—villanous looking fellows, mounted on miserable old hack-horses blindfolded, and so very poor that it was apparently with considerable difficulty that they supported their riders. These *picadórs* carried long spears in their hands, and were attired in fanciful livery bedizened with tarnished lace and faded ribbons. Their legs were encased in leather breeches stuffed with some impenetrable material to protect them from the horns of the bulls, giving them the clumsy look of a jackbooted postillion. These men are a necessary appendage to this species of amusement—a kind of "forlorn hope," being compelled to bear the brunt and danger of the contest. Next in order were the *chúlos* or combatants on foot, fantastically dressed and carrying in their hands barbed arrows, javelins, and other instruments of torture, to be used on the occasion. After these, came the *matadórs* or killers, with their long slender basket-hilted swords, which they use to terminate the existence of the unfortunate bulls when they can no longer afford amusement to the spectators. These *matadórs* are sometimes men of considerable celebrity in their profession, and are by far the most skilful of the different combatants. They are often regularly educated to the profession in their youth, and some of them are graduates of the old Castilian schools of Tauromachy. Last in the procession, was a mule-team, gaily caparisoned, and animated by the sound of tinkling bells around their necks, which was employed to drag the slaughtered animals from the arena. The procession passed around the ring to salute the captain-general, and the other dignitaries present, and to receive the congratulations of the expectant multitude; and then, all but the *chúlos* and two or three of the *picadórs* left the inclosure.

The trumpet again sounded, the gates were thrown open, and a large native bull rushed into the amphitheatre, amid the shouts of the enthusiastic spectators, who waved their hats, handkerchiefs, and scarfs, in a perfect frenzy of excitement and exultation. The noble animal appeared, at first, bewildered, and apparently undecided how to act. He turned his head in every direction, and scanned his foes, who were drawn up in battle array at the further side of the ring. Soon he began to snuff the air, lash his sides with his tail, and tear up the ground with his hoofs. At length, with a sudden bound, he rushed furiously against the nearest *picadór*, who sat on his trembling Rozinante with his lance in his hand, poised and ready to strike. The sharp weapon pierced the bull's neck, and kept him for a moment at bay. The withdrawal of the lance was followed by a stream of blood which deluged the ground. The bull then retreated to the opposite side of the ring, turned his face towards his enemies, and appeared as if he were disposed to act on the defensive. Several *toréros* now approached him from different directions; the one in front engaged his attention by flashing in his face a red scarf or shawl, while the others pierced his sides with small javelins, which were left to rankle in the flesh. This guerilla mode of warfare so exasperated the animal, that he turned on his tormentors, who hastily retreated behind the barriers. He then made for the nearest *picadór*, and thrusting his sharp horns into the horse's belly, lifted from the ground both horse and rider, and turned them completely over—the luckless *picadór* underneath. The enraged bull was with difficulty drawn off, and the wounded man dragged from under the horse, which lay struggling in the agonies of death. The bull again retreated; the purple gore streamed from gaping wounds, and his body was covered all over with sweat and foam. Worn down by the struggle, weary and faint from loss of blood, he soon began to writhe and tremble from weakness.

Another blast from the trumpet brought into the inclosure a *matadór* to try his "'prentice hand" at killing, for the bull was now to be despatched. But the fellow proved to be a mere novice, and made several unsuccessful attempts to inflict a mortal wound, which elicited a storm of groans and hisses from the angry spectators, who would not cease until he retired from the arena. Soon a favorite *matadór* was announced, who sprang into the ring and gracefully bowed amid the cheers and loud *vivas* of the excited multitude. He was slightly yet symmetrically formed, and as agile and graceful in his movements as a French dancing-master. He wore a cap of black velvet, with a sable plume, and a close-fitting jacket, which was profusely ornamented with gilt and embroidery, while a crimson scarf girded his almost feminine waist. As soon as the acclamations of the audience ceased, the *matadór* approached the bull, which had apparently regained a portion of his former vigor, notwithstanding his recent depletion, and shaking a scarf in his face, so excited the rage of the animal that he made a plunge at the intrepid Spaniard, who received him on the point of his sword, and buried it to the hilt between his shoulders. The bull gave one convulsive spring, carrying the sword in his body, and almost instantly expired. The whole audience arose simultaneously, and amid the plaudits and congratulations of the men, and a shower of bouquets from the ladies, the delighted *matadór*, with his hand on his heart, bowed himself out of the inclosure. Then the four-mule team, which was so conspicuous in the opening procession, reappeared, and the dead carcasses of the horse and bull were dragged from the arena amid the music of the band and the shouts of the jubilant multitude.

During our stay, several other bulls were brought in and attacked in a similar manner, with but slight variation in the details; and a horse was killed or fatally wounded at every encounter. Some of the bulls were more fierce than the one I have just described; others were not so valiant, but appeared to be frightened at the discordant noise of the populace, and would not come to the attack. In that case, a *chúlo* approached, and shook his red scarf in the face of the bull to inspire him, if possible, with pugnacious sentiments. Should this fail to produce the desired effect, they would launch at him numerous projectiles —in shape like a javelin—to the barbed point of which is attached a detonating preparation, which explodes the moment it penetrates the flesh of the animal, causing him to plunge, and writhe, and bellow in agony. Some would tear frantically around the arena, throw themselves on the ground, and try in every possible way to detach these instruments of torture, which were burning and rankling in their flesh; "the smoke of their torment" filling the air, and adding to the horror of the scene. Any extraordinary manifestation of suffering on the part of the poor persecuted animal was provocative of loud laughter and boisterous merriment from the spectators, many of whom seemed really to delight in its sufferings.

Becoming disgusted with the brutal and senseless

exhibition, we left some time before it was concluded. I was desirous of retiring during the first intermission; but my friends prevailed on me to remain a little longer, hoping that time would develop some new and more attractive feature in the exhibition. It is strange that any person possessing the ordinary feelings of humanity can tolerate such acts of cruelty; and that females of apparent delicacy and refinement can witness and take pleasure in such brutal spectacles, is, to me, perfectly unaccountable. It is certainly an indication that the finer and better feelings of their natures are blunted, and their sensibilities impaired, if their morals are not corrupted.

A few evenings since, I attended a theatrical exhibition on board of the Potomac, got up by the officers and crew for their own amusement. There were thirty or forty visitors present, who, with the crew, made quite a large audience. It was a very creditable and highly interesting amateur performance, although I believe that two or three of the actors on this occasion had once been connected with the stage. The first play on the programme was the historical drama of "Charles XII." This was followed by an original

Ethiopian extravaganza, in which the "excruciating opera" and the "high-falutin' ballet" were successfully burlesqued. During the intermission, a few of us were invited into the officers' cabin to partake of liquid refreshments and cigars. The evening's entertainment ended with an amusing farce, written by one of the crew, in which were introduced some hits of a local nature that were highly enjoyed by the audience.

It was past the "noon of night" before we all reached the shore, having to be rowed in small boats for nearly a mile. I enjoyed the trip exceedingly, as the evening was serene and beautiful, the air soft and balmy, and the full-orbed silver moon was high in the heavens, with her bright face mirrored in the deep waters of the quiet bay over which we were noiselessly gliding. The phosphorescent light emitted by the water, as our boat ruffled its placid surface, with flakes of silver dropping from the oars, and the trailing wake of silvery effulgence we left behind, was to me a novel and exceedingly beautiful sight. * * *

In closing my crude and desultory remarks concerning this land "ordained of Heaven the fairest spot on earth," I cannot do better than express the sentiments of a writer of some note, who has recently visited this country and given his impressions to the public.* He says:—

"If it were possible to contemplate only the beauties that nature has so prodigally lavished on this Eden of the Gulf, shutting out all that man has done and is still doing to mar the blessings of Heaven, then a residence in Cuba would present a succession of unalloyed pleasures equal to a poet's dream. But it is impossible, even if it would be desirable, to exclude the dark side of the picture. The American traveller, keenly alive to the social and political aspects of life, appreciates in full force the evils that challenge his observation at every step, and in every view which he may take. If he contrasts the natural scenery with the familiar pictures of home, he cannot help also contrasting the political condition of the people with that of his own country. The existence, almost under the shadow of the flag of the freest institutions the earth ever knew, of a government as purely despotic as that of the autocrat of the Russias, is a monstrous fact that

* "History of Cuba, by M. M. Ballou;" to which I am indebted for much valuable statistical information relative to that country.

startles the most indifferent observer. It must be seen to be realized.

"To go hence to Cuba, is not merely passing over a few degrees of latitude in a few days' sail,—it is a step from the nineteenth century back into the dark ages. In the clime of sun and endless summer, we are in the land of starless political darkness. Lying under the lee of a land where every man is a sovereign, is a realm where the lives, liberties, and fortunes of all are held at the tenure of the will of a single individual, and whence not a single murmur of complaint can reach the ear of the nominal ruler more than a thousand leagues away in another hemisphere. In close proximity to a country where the taxes, self-imposed, are so light as to be almost unfelt, is one where each free family pays nearly four hundred dollars per annum for the support of a bigoted tyranny, yielding in the aggregate an annual revenue of twenty-five millions of dollars, for which they receive no equivalent, no representation, no utterance—for pen and tongue are alike proscribed—no honor, no office, no emolument; where their industry is crippled, their intercourse with other nations hampered in every way, their bread literally snatched from their lips, the freedom of education denied, and every generous, liberal aspiration of the human soul stifled in its birth. Such are the contrasts, broad and striking, and such the reflections forced upon the mind of the citizen of the United States in Cuba." * * *

LETTER XIII.

KEY WEST, FLA., *April*, 1856.

MY last yarn was spun about two weeks since in Havana, just before my departure for the island-city, where I am now sojourning. I was "taken in" by our friends the H——s immediately on my arrival, and assigned a large airy room in their pleasant family mansion, where I am now fairly domesticated, and in the enjoyment of many comforts to which I have long been a stranger. Kind friends, pleasant weather, and a delightful climate, would have rendered my sojourn here particularly agreeable, had I not experienced a return of my old malady, inflammation of the stomach. My sufferings were intense, both day and night, and I became so weak from pain and loss of sleep that I could scarcely walk to the beach, a few rods distant. My nervous system was in such a state,

that I could not bear the least noise or excitement.
A loud voice, the crying of a child, the barking of a
dog, and even the sound of the surging sea—which
usually is music to my ear—now caused me sensations approaching, at times, almost to agony. I am
more than ever convinced that those who suffer from
a derangement of the nervous system do not usually
receive the sympathy they deserve; for it is a disease,
in my opinion, worse than all the ills to which flesh
is heir. But, thank Heaven, I am now better, or I
could not write, much less indite, this letter. * * *

Key West, formerly called by the Spaniards *Cayo
Hueso*, or Bone Key, is the most important of a chain
of small islands, or keys as they are termed, lying on
the southern coast of Florida. These islands are very
numerous, and vary in extent from the fractional part
of an acre to several miles. They are of coral formation—the work of small insects, who, however, cease
their labors as soon as they come to the surface of the
water. The entire growth above the water is dependent on other causes. A bunch of floating sea-weed,
or a loose spar from some dismantled vessel, may rest
upon this coral foundation. This is seized upon by

Coral Insects. 191

the industrious insects, who weave on the under side a net-work of coral, thus securing it permanently to the rock below. The slight elevation becomes gradually covered with sand or earth, forming the first rudiments of a soil. Some weary sea-bird, perhaps seeking a momentary resting-place, drops on the soil a seed, which takes root, blossoms, and bears fruit. Years after, other birds may rest in the branches of this isolated tree or shrub, and perchance scatter the seeds of other and different plants, which spring up, produce fruit, and are in their turn disseminated. The coral insects keep at work, enlarging the foundation to correspond with the increase of vegetation, until acres and perhaps miles of territory are formed in the midst of the ocean. Some of these islands increase in size each year, while others gradually diminish. This is said to be caused by the tidal currents, which pass through these intricate channels, in their tortuous course washing away portions of one island and transferring the loosened soil to another.

Key Largo lies near the main land, and is the largest of these numerous islands, being about twenty-five miles long, and from one to five miles wide.

Key West, although the third or fourth in size, is the only one of commercial importance. It has been designated as "the Key of the Gulf," and is the most southerly extremity of the United States. It is sixty miles south-west from Cape Sable, and ninety miles north of Havana, and is the only safe anchorage for vessels between those places. The island itself is four miles long and one mile wide, and its highest elevation is less than twenty feet above the level of the ocean. The harbor is capacious, and is defended by Fort-Taylor, a large and costly fortification, now in process of erection. Key West has also a military and naval hospital, and a number of barracks for soldiers, and is destined to be a place of considerable importance. The steamer Isabel, which carries the mail between Charleston and Havana, touches here once a week, and is about the only means of communication with the main land. Arrangements are now being made, I learn, to have the California steamers coal here, and take in supplies on their return voyage.

The town is situated on the west end of the island, and is dignified by the title of city, although having less than three thousand inhabitants. It is, however,

A Paradise for Wreckers.

the most populous place in Florida Being a sea-port town, the society is unavoidably miscellaneous. The permanent residents are principally Americans, English, Spaniards, and Bahamians, with a large infusion of slaves and free blacks. These Bahamians, known here by the peculiar sobriquet of "conchs," are quite numerous, amounting to at least one-fifth of the entire population. They have a settlement by themselves in the outskirts of the city, and subsist mainly by fishing, gathering sponges, and giving assistance to wrecked vessels. Large quantities of sponges are annually collected by these amphibious bipeds, who seem to be as much at home in the water as out of it.

The southern coast of Florida is very much feared by navigators, on account of its numerous shoals and reefs, its labyrinthine channels, and the treacherous under current of the Gulf-stream in the vicinity. It is said that about fifty vessels are annually wrecked on this coast, and the inhabitants of Key West derive a large revenue from this source. There are a great number of wrecking merchants in this city, most of whom have acquired fortunes in the business. I have always looked upon wrecking as a nefarious occupation, a kind of *quasi* piracy; but I am assured by reliable citizens here, that it is generally conducted upon equitable rules, for the mutual benefit of all parties interested, and that many lives and much valuable property are saved every year by the exertions of these wreckers. A large number of vessels, and quite an army of seamen, are now engaged in the business, and nearly all of the inhabitants on this island are, directly or indirectly, interested in it.

On the east end of the island are a number of salt-water ponds, where salt is made by solar evaporation. These works have been destroyed several times by gales, and the manufacture of salt for a while suspended. They are now in successful operation, and yield about two hundred thousand bushels annually. The present owner, Mr. C. W. Dennis, came here from Alabama, a few years ago, for his health. The salt air and equable climate proved so beneficial to him, that he has continued to reside here ever since. Mr. Dennis is a gentleman of wealth, with a decided taste for literary and scientific pursuits, to which he devotes a large portion of his time. I am indebted to him for much valuable information relative to the commerce and agricultural capabilities of this island, and for many interesting facts concerning the numerous keys and islands in this vicinity.

The climate of Key West is delightful. The island is constantly visited by invigorating sea-breezes, and is never so intensely hot as some parts of Cuba. The mean temperature is 75°; the mercury seldom rises above 85°, and has never been known to fall below 43° since the island has been inhabited. This would be a paradise for invalids, with its perpetual summer, its balmy, health-giving atmosphere, and its ever-verdant foliage, were there a greater variety of land scenery, more pleasant drives, and better hotel accommodations. But it is sadly deficient in all of these hygeian requisites. The greater part of the island is uncultivated, being covered with dwarfish trees and scraggy underbrush. The soil, in many places, is overspread to the depth of several inches with loose beach sand, carried there by the heavy gales which occasionally sweep over the island. After the novelty of the place has worn off, and the invalid visitor has become weary of gazing on the broad and monotonous ocean which surrounds him on every side, he will,

I imagine, experience a feeling of loneliness—an oppressive sensation, as if he were in too contracted and confined a place; and this could not be otherwise than unfavorable to his restoration to health. Were it not for these few drawbacks, Key West would be one of the most desirable places for a winter residence on this continent.

The soil is thin, and apparently almost sterile, yet the heat of the climate and the soft tropical air make every kind of vegetation flourish. It is particularly adapted to fruit. Many kinds, such as oranges, cocoa-nuts, tamarinds, bananas, olives, dates, and others peculiar to the tropics, grow here almost spontaneously, and might be cultivated with profit, were it not for the great cost of inclosing and preparing the land. I was shown several varieties of plants introduced here from Mexico by the late Dr. Henry Perrine, more than twenty years ago, which had become thoroughly domesticated. One variety of the agave family, named by Dr. Perrine *Agave sisalana*, has been very widely disseminated here, and is now growing freely on the island. This valuable plant produce what is known to the commercial world as Sisal hemp.

It is stronger and more durable than the celebrated Manilla hemp, a single fibre having been known to sustain a weight of six pounds, and is exceedingly valuable for cordage and other purposes. If a suitable machine could be invented for removing the pulp and cleansing the fibre, it would soon become an important and profitable article of commerce. The plant will flourish on poor thin soil. For that reason, if no other, it is especially adapted to many parts of southern Florida, and the islands bordering on the gulf.

During my stay at Key West, I had the pleasure of conversing with several persons who had been intimately acquainted with Dr. Perrine, and they regarded the enterprise in which he was engaged at the time of his death* of incalculable importance to

---

* On the 7th day of August, 1840, an attack was made on Indian Key, a small island on the southern coast of Florida, by a band of Seminole Indians, and several of the inhabitants massacred. "Among those who fell victims to Indian rapacity and ferocity was Dr. Henry Perrine, a gentleman of distinguished talents and education, who had temporarily settled himself with his family at Indian Key for the purpose of introducing the culture of the tea-plant and other exotics into the territory of Florida. Dr. Perrine had intended to settle on a township of land situated near Cape Florida: but in consequence of

this country. The object of the association of which Dr. Perrine was the originator, was " to encourage the introduction and promote the cultivation of tropical plants in the United States." It was the intention of the parties to introduce such valuable exotics as would grow on comparatively sterile soil, and to make available a large part of southern Florida, now of no real value to our government, thus increasing the national wealth and the prosperity of our common country.

Dr. Perrine was an able and enthusiastic botanist, and during the ten or twelve years that he was American Consul at Campeachy and Tobasco, he devoted himself to the domestication of tropical

the Seminole war, which was then raging, he was not allowed to carry his designs into execution. A township of land was granted to him in the year 1838 by Congress, with a view to the encouragement of his favorite enterprise. While waiting patiently for the close of the war, at Indian Key, a place of supposed perfect security, a band of savages landed on the island, desolated it, and assassinated a portion of the inhabitants: and among those who fell was Dr. Perrine."— *From the National Intelligencer.*

The particulars of this massacre and of the escape of Dr. Perrine's family will be given at the close of this chapter.

Domestication of Tropical Plants. 199

plants in the United States, by patient collections and persevering transmissions of valuable seeds and plants, and by procuring the necessary information for their culture. Among the plants he introduced (many of which would without doubt have been successfully cultivated, had he lived) were several varieties of the palm, the agave, the tea-plant, the coffee-shrub, the rich dyes and precious woods of Mexico, the various spices of the Indies, and the delicious fruits of Tropical America. There are now on exhibition at the Patent Office in Washington samples of a nankeen-colored cotton, and of a drab vegetable silk, sent there by Dr. P., which have excited considerable interest among botanists, and persons engaged in the manufacture of those commodities.

When on my way to Cuba, I met with a gentleman engaged in the government coast survey, who had recently visited Matacumba and other small islands in the immediate vicinity of Indian Key, and I learned from him that the island of Matacumba was covered with trees and shrubs, different from any to be found on the main land, or on any of the islands near by. They were, in all probability, introduced there by Dr. Perrine, who, during his residence at Indian Key, used this island as a nursery for the cultivation and propagation of exotic trees and plants.

NARRATIVE OF THE MASSACRE AT INDIAN KEY.

The circumstances attending the death of Dr. Perrine, as related by members of his family, are as follows:—In the year 1838, Congress granted to him a township of land in southern Florida for the purpose of introducing and acclimating valuable tropical plants. During the winter of that year, Dr. P., with his family, consisting of his wife, two daughters, and a son, took up his residence at Indian Key, a small island lying about twenty miles south from Cape Sable, to await the termination of the Seminole war, before removing to the main land. While there, the Doctor occupied himself in preparing a nursery of exotic plants on the uninhabited island of Matacumba near by, intending, as soon as the war was over, to remove them to his township on the main land. The few families residing at Indian Key had no apprehension of an attack from the Indians, who, it was presumed, would not venture so far away from their secure retreat among the everglades. Their supposed security was rendered more certain, from the fact, evidently known to the Indians, that a number of United States soldiers were stationed at Tea Table Key, less than two miles distant.

Indian Key, at this time, contained a dozen or more dwellings, two or three warehouses, and one store, with an area of about twelve acres. The house occupied by Dr. Perrine was the largest on the island. It was three stories high, including the attic, with a piazza at one end, and cupola on the top; and was built so close to the sea, that during high tide three sides of the house were surrounded by water. Fronting the piazza, and extending into the ocean, was a short wharf or pier, used for unloading wood and family supplies; between it and the house was a narrow covered passage, walled up on each side. The wharf itself was constructed of posts driven into the ground and covered over with timber and plank. The space under the wharf was used as a pen for turtles, and known as "a turtle crawl." It communicated with the cellar by the narrow passage before mentioned, at the outer end of which was a row of palmetto posts driven into the soft marl, far enough apart to freely admit the tide, but not to allow the escape of the turtles. The cellar under the house being open to the influx of the sea, was used by the family as a place for bathing, the water being four or five feet deep during high-tide, but receding as the tide ebbed, so as to leave but a few inches on the bottom. The bathing-place was entered by a trap-door from the dressing-room above.

This slight description of the island, with the location and arrangement of the house occupied by Dr. Perrine, will enable the reader the better to understand the events set forth in the following narrative.

On the morning of the 7th of August, 1840, between two and three o'clock, the family of Dr. Perrine were aroused from their slumbers by the discharge of guns, crashing of glass, and the fearful yells of Indians, who had approached the island so stealthily as to escape observation. The Doctor sprang from his hammock, where he had been watching the sick-bed of his eldest daughter who had been ill of a fever for several weeks, caught her up in his arms, and followed by his wife and other daughter in their night dresses, started down stairs to seek a place of concealment. At this moment they discovered that the son, a lad of thirteen, was not with them; they found him in his room in another part of the building, and hurriedly descended to the dressing-room at the foot of the stairs. Here the Doctor left his family and went to another room for his fire-arms, having in the house at the time one of Colt's revolving rifles, three of Allen's six-shooters, and one double-barrelled shot-gun. He had plenty of powder and balls, but to his dismay found that he was out of percussion caps, which rendered his fire-arms useless as a means of defence. Somewhat discouraged, but not without hope, the Doctor—finding the yard and piazza filled with Indians, and no possibility of escape in that direction—opened the trap-door leading to the bathing-room below, as the safest place of refuge, and told his family to descend and "he would go back and see what could be done." They did as he requested, and were soon immersed to the waist in water, and surrounded by darkness and gloom. They groped their way into the narrow passage leading to the "turtle crawl," where their further progress was intercepted by the palmetto posts before mentioned. Here they remained in darkness and suspense, awaiting the husband and father whom they were never to see again in this world.

The Indians had by this time reached the rear of the house and were crowded upon the piazza, but a few feet above the heads of the affrighted family, firing their guns into the windows, yelling, and battering away at the door. During a slight cessation of the noise, they heard Dr. Perrine from the upper piazza, calling to the Indians in Spanish, informing them that he was a physician. This was all they could understand, as the Indians immediately gave a loud shout, and apparently left the premises. In a few moments Dr. Perrine came down stairs, closed the trap-door leading to the cellar, and drew over it a large chest of seeds to conceal it from observation. This noble, self-sacrificing act—the last he ever performed for his family—undoubtedly saved their lives.

Dr. Perrine had many important papers and manuscripts, the fruits of years of toil and research, which were of incalculable value to him, and which he was desirous of saving. Knowing that the Indians were friendly to the Spaniards, and trusting to his knowledge of the Spanish language, which he spoke like a native, and to their known desire to secure the services of a white physician, he was confident that he could prevail on them to spare his dwelling, and the lives of himself and family, and that he would ultimately be able to save many of his valuable papers. This idea is borne out by the subsequent occurrences of that fatal night.

A short time after the Indians had left the house, the trembling listeners heard the rattling of a chain as it was dropped into a small boat which had been fastened to the wharf, but a few yards from where they were concealed, and cautious footsteps in the water. They afterwards learned that Mr. Charles Howe, who now resides at Key West, then made his escape with all his family. Shortly after, they heard the Indians breaking into the different houses near by, and from their loud discordant yells it was evident that they had obtained access to the store, and were now maddened by intoxication. Despair seized on the terrified inmates of this half submerged prison-house, as they heard the returning footsteps of the Indians, who now began a furious assault upon the dwelling, and with the aid of sticks of wood that were piled on the wharf, soon battered down the door and effected an entrance. For a time they seemed to be more intent on breaking windows, destroying furniture, and securing plunder, than searching for victims. At last a voice was heard to say in English " they're all hid"—" old man up-stairs." A rush was then made evidently in that direction, and in a few moments the sound of heavy blows was heard apparently upon a massive trap-door that led to the cupola, where it was supposed the Doctor had retreated for safety. Soon they heard a terrific crash as the door gave way, followed by a single rifle shot, and then the loud war-whoops and demoniac yells of the savages indicated their success and the massacre of Dr. Perrine. For a long time afterwards the terror-stricken fugitives heard the Indians dragging trunks and other articles of plunder over their heads, and loading them into boats. Once, as the turtles made a noise in the water, an Indian raised one of the planks and looked down, but fortunately not towards the end where the family were secreted.

Anxiously the trembling inmates of this gloomy

hiding-place awaited the approach of light, which they hoped would bring succor and relief, as they supposed these ruthless invaders would then leave the island. As the day began to dawn, they could see through the crevices of their place of retreat boats passing by loaded with spoils, and hear the cry of the marauders close at hand. Soon they heard the sound of desultory firing; then came the booming of a cannon, which was followed by prolonged yells of defiance. Hope began to animate their breasts, and they waited with feverish anxiety other indications of the approach of succor. But the firing ceased, and the looked-for aid came not. It was afterwards ascertained that nearly all the soldiers stationed at Tea-Table Key had been sent away a few days before on a naval expedition, and those left behind were in the hospital, and not considered fit for active service. When it was known at the Key that the Indians had made an attack on this island, a few partly-disabled soldiers procured a small boat, in which they placed two four-pound swivels, and as soon as it was light started out for the purpose of trying to intercept the Indians and cut off their retreat to the main land. In the hurry of their departure, they unfortunately took with them six-pound cartridges instead of four, and at the first discharge the overloaded guns recoiled so violently that they went overboard, and the soldiers had to retreat, to avoid being captured. The Indians followed them for some distance, firing at them, and killing or severely wounding one of their number.

It soon became evident to Mrs. Perrine and her children that the house was on fire, as smoke began to make its way slowly into their place of concealment. It was some time, however, before it proved troublesome, as the building was fired near the cupola, and had to burn downwards. But as its devouring progress was not stayed, it soon found its way to the lower floor, when the smoke became stifling, and so dense that they could scarcely see themselves, although clasped in each other's arms. The tide had now ebbed, leaving but a few inches of water over the bottom. To escape suffocation, they lay with their faces close to the water, splashed it around them to keep the air in motion, and breathed through the folds of their wet night-clothes. At length the timbers above their heads caught fire, and tongues of angry flame darted out, and were choked back by wet marl in the hands of the terror-stricken captives, whose doom seemed now to be sealed. No escape was left for them towards the house, as the mouth of their retreat looked like a great oven or fiery furnace, and in front of them was a row of piles driven deep into the marl and spiked at the top. In a few moments the burning building fell into the cellar with a fearful crash. The boy screamed out in terror, as a horrible death by fire seemed inevitable. His mother and sister endeavored to stop his cries, fearing the Indians would hear him; but he declared "that he would rather be killed than burned to death," and broke away from them. In his frantic efforts to escape, he forced his way between two palmetto posts, one of which had been loosened at the top, and escaped into the turtle-pen, whence he made his way to the outside of the wharf.

His mother and sisters remained for a short time in agonizing suspense, thinking that he would be killed or taken prisoner by the Indians, and their discovery would be certain. But hearing no noise, and knowing that they would be burned to death if they remained where they were, the mother *dug down into the marl with her hands* to the bottom of a post, and by an almost superhuman effort succeeded in displacing it sufficiently to admit the passage of herself and daughters. As they went forward under the wharf, on which were several cords of wood on fire, the live coals fell on their bare heads and shoulders; but they heeded them not, being so overjoyed at having escaped from the horrible death which but a few moments before seemed to be their doom. Joyfully they inhaled the pure air once more, and with grateful hearts thanked God for their deliverance. With slow and cautious footsteps they made their way through the shallow water to the outside of the wharf, looking anxiously around for the son, of whose fate they were ignorant, and trying to discover some place of security where they could remain until rescued.

Let us now for a moment follow the son after his escape from beneath the burning wharf. Seeing a fleet of canoes, nearly a mile distant, filled with Indians, and supposing that they had all left the island, he started in the direction of one of the buildings not destroyed, hoping to find some person who would go to the relief of his mother and sisters. But no human being was visible, and no sound heard, except the crackling of the flames of the nearly consumed dwelling he had so recently occupied, and of the burning wood on the wharf. He passed in front of the store, the door of which was open, little dreaming that at the moment several drunken Indians were within, collecting the few spoils not taken away by those who had left the island. Retracing his steps, he approached the spot where his mother and sisters were incarcerated, in the expectation of never seeing them again, as the wharf above their late place of concealment was all on fire, and their escape at that time would have been impossible. As he cast his eyes despairingly in that direction, to his great surprise and joy he beheld them emerging from the turtle-pen. He ran to meet them, and as he passed the landing near the store, he discovered a boat partly loaded with goods, evidently belonging to the Indians then in the building. When he reached the family, his mother was supporting in her arms her invalid daughter, who, becoming faint from weakness and fatigue, had sunk down, and was begging her mother and sister to leave her and make their escape, as "she said she was dying and could go no further." But they succeeded in dragging her through the water to the boat, which they unloosed from its fastening, and with the aid of one oar and a pole contrived to push it out into the open sea.

Their escape was truly providential; for, had they been a few moments earlier or later in getting to the boat, they would, in all probability, have been discovered by the Indians, who had partly filled the boat with goods, and had gone back to the store for more plunder. Seeing a vessel at anchor a short distance from Tea-Table Key, the son took off his shirt, and fastening it to a pole, hoisted it as a signal of distress. Twice they got aground, but the boy having been accustomed to managing a boat got her off with but slight detention. They had proceeded about half a mile when they discovered two Indians in a canoe just starting out in pursuit of them; but seeing a boat approaching from the direction of the vessel, the Indians returned and set fire to the store and the few remaining buildings. The fugitives were taken up by a boat from the schooner Medium, which vessel they reached about noon—some ten hours from the time the attack was first made on the island. They found on board several of the inhabitants of the Key who had escaped during the night, and among them the family of Mr. Howe, their neighbors and intimate friends. The captain of the vessel was very kind to the ladies, provided them with sheets in lieu of dresses, and made them as comfortable as could be expected under the circumstances. Mrs. Perrine and her children were almost destitute of clothing, and in a nearly exhausted state. Their night-garments were in tatters; their hands sore from digging up the marl to protect their heads from the heat of the burning building; their shoulders smarting from contact with falling coals; and their faces blistered from long exposure to the scorching rays of a tropical noon-day sun reflected in a sea of polished glass.

The next day Mr. Howe, with a few men from the schooner, returned to the island, gathered together the bones of Dr. Perrine from the ruins of his dwelling, and buried them under the broad spreading leaves of one of his favorite agaves on the beautiful island of Lower Matacumba, where perpetual summer reigns, and "fragrance ever clothes the flow'ring earth."

"Peace to the dust that in silence reposes,
   Beneath the dark shade of the cypress and yew:
Let spring deck the spot with the earliest roses,
   And heaven wash the leaves with its holiest dew."

The family remained on board of the schooner until the afternoon of the next day, when they were transferred to "The Flirt," a United States vessel-of-war commanded by Capt. McLaughlin, who gave up his state-room to the ladies, and rendered them all the assistance in his power. The invalid daughter was carried on board on a cot, being too ill to stand; but with careful nursing, and the skilful attendance of the ship's surgeon, Dr. Taliaferro, she soon began to improve in health and strength. The Flirt proceeded to Cape Florida, where she remained about a week, until the arrival of the steamer Santee, in which vessel the family took passage for St. Augustine under the care and protection of Dr. Edward Worrel, of the Army, who very kindly accompanied them to their friends at the North.

LETTER XIV.

SAVANNAH, *April*, 1856.

I LEFT Key West by the steamer Isabel late on the afternoon of the 16th instant, for this city. The day was lovely, the air balmy, the sky brilliant, and the sun as bright as ever gladdened a tropical landscape. Old Ocean himself was in the best of humors, his broad expansive face was placid and serene, and everything indicated a pleasant voyage. The deck of the steamer was crowded with passengers, most of whom were from the North, who had been seeking health and recreation in a warmer clime, and were now returning to their homes, willing to exchange the cloudless sky and balmy atmosphere of the sunny South for the more substantial comforts of home, and the companionship of kindred and friends.

> "There is a magic in the name of home,
>   Felt in the spirit's yearnings; man may roam
>   Careering on his wild and thoughtless way,
>   Yet in all his wanderings is still within
>   The attractive influence of that sunny spot,
>   Home, sweet home!"

I was fortunate in meeting with a number of ladies and gentlemen whose acquaintance I had made in Cuba, and our greeting was as cordial as if we had known each other for years. It was really a pleasant reunion, which we celebrated on deck, in relating our individual experiences since we parted at Cuba. The evening was surpassingly lovely; the sun had gone to his rest surrounded by a halo of golden effulgence; and his pale-faced sister, the crescent moon, was inconspicuous amid her innumerable progeny of bright and twinkling stars which bedecked

> "——— Night's dark pavilion,
>   Spread wide o'er the wasteful deep."

What can be more beautiful than a starry night on the ocean; with naught but heaven above, heaven around, and heaven reflected in the water beneath.

It is one vast sea of splendor, boundless in space, and glorious in its illuminings. We remained on deck enjoying the scene before us—the jewelled firmament above, the balmy atmosphere around, and the silver-crested waves beneath breaking with gentle music against the sharp prow of our vessel as she flew over the water—until midnight was upon us and admonished us to retire.

My state-room companion was a Lieutenant in the Army, who was on his way to Washington to receive orders. He was an intelligent and agreeable young man, about twenty-five years of age, and moreover, modest and unassuming; which virtues are so rare among gentlemen of his profession that I take pleasure in noticing the fact. We laid ourselves upon our respective shelves and gossipped about things terrestrial until sleep weighed down my eyelids and steeped my senses in forgetfulness. I slept soundly until about daylight, when I was awakened by the accelerated motion of the vessel, as if that blustering vagabond Boreas were trying to provoke the aqueous elements to wrath; unconscious, perhaps, that by so doing he would be very likely to excite the *bile* in us.

Sleep was now out of the question, and I lay rolling and tumbling about in my berth until the morning watch was called, when I got up, and meandering to the deck, witnessed a scene of unsurpassed grandeur and sublimity. Alas! what a change had come over the spirit of his Oceanic Majesty since I left the deck but a few hours before. Then he was

—— "As meek, and mild,
And gentle as an unweaned child."

Now, he was dashing and splashing, rearing and tearing, with impetuous fury; his hitherto serene countenance was writhed and distorted, and he was lashing the sides of our gallant vessel with angry vehemence. I *sickened* at the sight, and hastily retreated to the cabin. Here the sound of the breakfast-bell fell discordantly on my ear, neither was it in harmony with the *tone* of my stomach. To me it was a mournful sound—a knell to my departed appetite—a requiem over lost joys and buried hopes. The captain suggested tea and toast as a sedative, and led the way to the breakfast-room. I followed "like a lamb to the slaughter." My limbs obeyed, but my stomach rebelled. I reached the table, which was nearly unoccupied, but profusely covered with tempting viands; wondered they did not fall off *when the table rose to meet me;* managed to sit down, the chair being fastened, drank one spoonful of tea, which was nauseous, and the toast was anything but appetising. They passed a plate of hot steak under my nose; I could stand it no longer, but dropping my knife and fork hastily mounted the stairs, lest I might leave *something on my plate not in the bill of fare.* The cool air revived me. I began to take courage, and manfully resolved to walk the deck and banish such *idle fancies.* Proudly I arose; the vessel rose with me; she careened, I careened also; she plunged, and I suppose that I must have "followed suit," for I suddenly found myself on my knees at one end of the vessel, paying tribute to Neptune.

How I managed to reach my state-room I hardly know; but I *do* know that I remained there for twenty-four hours, suffering as I never suffered before. The nausea of sea-sickness I could endure; but such incessant, torturing, racking pains in my head I never before experienced; and the spasms in my stomach were at times so severe, that I almost feared that my "mortal fabric was about to be dissolved." I did not close my eyes in sleep until long after midnight, when nature became exhausted, and I relapsed into a state of forgetfulness. When I awoke the next morning, I had a few oranges brought to my room, which refreshed and invigorated me. I managed at breakfast to overcome my aversion to tea and toast, and a small piece of beef-steak was not unpalatable. Went on deck, found the aspect of nature changed, received the congratulations of friends, and your correspondent "was himself again." However, I am convinced more than ever that I have no stomach for the sea, and resolve for the *fourth* and last time, to confine my journeyings in future to terra-firma, or at least within sight of its genial shores.

It is Ralph Waldo Emerson, I believe, who says that "sea-life is an acquired taste, like that for tomatoes and olives." This may be the experience of some voyagers, but not of all. I háve tried a number of times to acquire a liking for the sea, but the oftener I make the attempt the greater is my aversion to the saline *condiment*, which invariably disturbs the equilibrium of my stomach. Poets, in the phrensy of inspiration, may sing rapturously of "a life on the ocean wave, and a home on the rolling deep;" but, much as I may admire the poetry and melody of the song, my feelings will not respond to the sentiment therein expressed. The recollections of my several experiences on ship-board are, I must say, provocative of any but agreeable sensations.

I have no objections to the sea in the prospective, when viewed from a comfortable position on dry land; it is, in fact, from such a stand-point, a sublime and beautiful sight. But I do object to being "cribbed, cabined, and confined" for an indefinite period in an uneasy vessel, where one is liable to be nauseated by the villanous effluvium of bilge-water, or half stifled with mephitic air, even if fortunate enough to escape the horrors of sea-sickness. Furthermore, to be subjected to the capricious humors and insolent pranks of that old salt-water god,—he of the trident, who delights in annihilating your appetite, turning your stomach inside out, and making you appear as if you were "half seas over" when you have just begun the voyage—is not only disagreeable, but extremely mortifying to one of my staid, sober, and strictly temperate habits.

Among our motley assemblage of passengers—some forty or fifty in number, and representing several different nations—were three or four, whose peculiarity of appearance or eccentricity of manner made them conspicuous. One individual, with a dark, sinister countenance, and heavy black beard, was pointed out to me as a Cuban millionaire, who was supposed to be engaged in the African slave-trade, and his great wealth the result of his accursed traffic in human flesh. A more morose and forbidding face I never saw on a human form. From beneath a heavy, overhanging brow, flashed *one* basilisk eye, as bright and coruscant as if the fire of a thousand furnaces were burning there. The other eye was invisible, being covered with a small black patch. If Blue-Beard ever existed except in the imaginations of credulous children, I think this individual must have been a lineal descendant, for he realized more fully my idea of that man-monster than any human being that I ever saw. Evidently desiring to escape observation, he sat most of the time alone, in a retired part of the vessel, smoking a richly ornamented pipe, of antique design; he was not seen at the public table, nor was he known to hold any conversation, or to have communication with any of the passengers.

Another individual, antipodal in every respect to the one just described, was, perhaps, fifty years of age, quite intelligent, well-dressed (although his clothes were beginning to look seedy), and evidently had seen much of the world. His good-natured face and *sans souci* manner were a card of introduction to most of the passengers, and had it not been for a predisposition which he evinced to indulge in the marvellous, he would have been a valuable acquisition to our floating society. I have, during my somewhat extensive intercourse with the world, observed human nature in a great variety of phases. I have seen talking politicians; talking poets—many of whom are decidedly *prosy;* talking lawyers—some of whom, like necessity, know no law; talking divines, and those of the fraternity *not* particularly divine; and last, but not least, talking women! With the exception of the latter (with whom, however, talking is the rule, not the exception), I never before saw so garrulous a biped as the one I am now describing. He talked incessantly. Where he had not been was not worth visiting; what he had not seen was not worth seeing; what he had not endured was not martyrdom. He had visited Europe, Asia, Africa, and the various islands of the ocean; had circumnavigated the globe, and *doubled many a horn.* He had picked up diamonds from Brazilian sands, and had his " pocket full of rocks " fresh from the mines of Australia. Had breakfasted on Mount Blanc, dined in the crater of Vesuvius, and supped on the Dead Sea; had slept amid the ruins of the Alhambra, drunk wine on the top of Pompey's Pillar, and bathed in the Hellespont; had hunted buffaloes on our western prairies, tigers in Bengal, and elephants in the jungles of Ceylon; had explored the Polar regions, and travelled over Sahara's desert waste. He knew every one, from his Holiness the Pope to the " King of the Cannibal Islands "—from the Czar of Russia to the Great Mogul himself—and enjoyed an intimate companionship with the seventh son of the world-renowned Baron Munchausen, whose adventures were but "small vegetables" compared with his more wonderful exploits.

Another personage attracted the notice of many of the passengers by his peculiar dialect, and exquisite cockney-air. He was a verdant sprig of the English upper-ten-dom, who was just emerging from a chrysalis state into an adolescent butterfly. This tender scion had but recently left his parental conservatory in Yorkshire—his speech being profusely interlarded with aspirated vowels and provincialisms—and was now abroad in search of a field in which to sow his wild oats. He was an exquisite of the "first water," who sported more airs than *hairs*, although an incipient moustache was beginning to shadow his lip, and a few downy hairs were faintly discernible on his effeminate chin. On the fore-finger of his right hand he wore a ring about the size of a Spanish quarter, which he ostentatiously displayed as he removed his cigar from his mouth and discoursed upon its delectable qualities. He smoked none but the most " hexpensive cigars," those manufactured " hespecially" for him by the celebrated Cabaña. He had considerable to say about the " governor"—meaning his paternal ancestor—who, it seemed, was very desirous that a tutor should accompany his son on his travels; to which the youth objected, imagining, no doubt, that it would be an impediment to his free and easy locomotion. He thought "Hamerica did very well for a new country, but it never would compare with ' Hold Hingland.'" During a conversation with one of the passengers, I heard him say something about "the nuptial haltar," evidently referring to the *noose* matrimonial, which is a halter to some, and a silken tie to others.

Speaking of matrimony, I am reminded of an amusing incident that occurred during the last day of our voyage. Among the passengers were a newly married couple whose disparity in age, and want of "spiritual affinity," were remarked by all who saw them. The gentleman was apparently on the downhill side of fifty, while the lady was young enough to be his daughter, even had he not been married until somewhat late in life. They were mated, but *not* matched; and joined together by the "iron bands of wedlock," not by the holy ties of mutual love and affection. There was evidently as much dissimilarity in their tastes and dispositions, as disparity in their ages. The husband was loving and devoted; the wife cold and indifferent. He was uxorious and demonstrative, while she was imperturbable, and at times almost ill-natured. Wherever she was, there he would surely be. If she remained on deck, he was by her side. If she went below, he followed her like a shadow. This continual watchfulness and unremitting attention were apparently annoying to her, and she spoke to him at times somewhat petulantly. Still, the good-natured and adoring husband did not relax in his attentions to his younger half, but tried to anticipate all her wants. One day, during an unusually heavy sea, she left her seat on the deck and hastily retreated to the cabin, followed by her husband. In a few moments he returned, with fright depicted in his countenance, and inquired for a doctor, saying that his wife "had been suddenly taken very ill, and he was afraid she was dying." The captain was called, and after making a few inquiries of the frightened husband, sent to his stateroom, not a physician but—*a chambermaid with a basin.* The finale of this ludicrous affair can readily be imagined by those at all familiar with nautical life. * * * * * *

LETTER XV.

Montgomery, Ala., *April,* 1856.

My last letter was written from the lovely metropolis of genial, warm-hearted Georgia, where I remained for three days, just long enough to view the city, and some of its suburban celebrities. To me, there is something balmy and healing associated with Savannah; its very name being suggestive of a peculiar feature of southern scenery. Providence intended it as a kind of familiar resting-place between the frigid North and the scorching Tropics; its mild, equable atmosphere preparing the cautious invalid for a transition to either of the two extremes.

The city lies about eighteen miles from the sea on the Savannah River, a stream of considerable importance which forms the dividing line between South Carolina and Georgia, and is of no inconsiderable magnitude, being navigable, during a part of the year, for vessels of large tonnage to Savannah, and for steamboats almost its entire length. The country bordering on the Carolina shore is low, level, and unattractive in appearance; but the soil is rich, easily irrigated, and well adapted to the cultivation of rice, which is the principal staple of the Palmetto State.

Savannah is situated on a sandy bluff or strip of table-land some thirty or forty feet above the level of the river, and has a population of twenty-four thousand, including free blacks and slaves. The streets are wide, and regularly laid out; with twenty-four public squares or parks, which are filled with shade trees, giving to the city a peculiarly rural aspect. Among the trees most noticeable were the noble live-oak; the curious mulberry; the modest elm; the fragrant magnolia, and the much admired Pride of India, which was just beginning to bloom.

This has been very aptly denominated "the city of shade and silence." It is certainly the most pensive, quiet, and sober-looking city that I have ever visited. The streets are all hushed and silent " 'neath the cloistered boughs" of umbrageous trees, the foliage being so dense that daylight is almost excluded; and what little remains, is softened down to a perpetual twilight. The sand is so deep in the streets that carriages pass along as noiselessly as gondolas in the canals of Venice. The few people to be seen out of doors, and the absence of that hum of business incident to most northern cities, render the stillness more deep and apparent. As you pass through the silent and almost deserted streets, you wish for a little more bustle and appearance of business. The quiet is really oppressive. You are not in a solitude, but surrounded by evidences of population; therefore, you feel the want of that hum incident to life, just as much as when wandering in the fields and groves, you long for the music of birds, the buzz of insects, or the sounds of running brooks and waving trees. A sabbath-day stillness prevails here at all times, and were it not that the shops and places of business are closed on that day, it would be difficult to tell when Sunday began or ended.

It is a noticeable fact that this city is destitute of any prominent thoroughfare—any one fashionable street for promenade and shopping—where, during pleasant weather, the butterflies of fashion can

> "Shop, and lounge, and gaze, and stare,
> And show themselves,—and take the air."

No *one* street that I saw, seemed to be pre-eminent. The few handsome shops and stores are so scattered about the city, that it has a decidedly rural aspect—more the appearance of a quiet country village, than of a commercial city. In one of the principal squares is a monument to General Greene, of Revolutionary fame. Another elegant monument is now being erected in Chippewa square, to the memory of Count Pulaski, a brave Polish officer who was killed during an attack on Savannah in 1779, when the city was in the possession of the English.

Savannah has many suburban attractions. The country around is pleasantly diversified with hill and valley, winding streams, and patches of wood-land. Just beyond the limits of the city is the "Laurel Grove Cemetery," a quiet, lovely spot, where flowers bloom upon grassy mounds, and vines planted by the hand of affection twine their tendrils around many a sculptured shrine where repose the loved ones whose memories are thus perpetuated.

"Oh! noiseless city of the mighty dead!
　Lonely and mute, yet are thy annals fraught
　With solemn teachings, and thy broad page spread
　　With the rich lore of soul-awakening thought."

Some five or six miles from here is the Cemetery of Buonaventura, one of the most solemn and appropriate burial-places imaginable. Nature has done more for the adornment of this spot than Art. It contains no elegant mausoleums, and but few monuments sufficiently conspicuous to attract the attention of the unobservant visitor. It is an immense grove of giant trees, or rather a succession of broad avenues, crossing each other at right angles, carpeted by a smooth greensward, and bordered with stately trees, whose farreaching branches are festooned with the sombre-hued moss peculiar to this climate. As far as the eye can reach are vistas of interwoven boughs; the pendent drapery in wild beauty wreathes the patriarchal oaks 'till the "mingled fret-work" seems like the embodiment of some vast cathedral aisle. There was something peculiarly attractive to me in the gloomy grandeur of this forest sanctuary; a weird, unearthly beauty in its silent groves; and the sighing breeze, mournful and dirge-like, as it was wafted through the shadowy aisles of Nature's cloister, served to lift the soul

> "Above the thoughts of earth, and give it power
> Nearer to commune with its kindred Heaven."

During the few days that I remained in Savannah, I had an opportunity to see something of the Georgia Cottonocracy, and to get an inkling of some of their peculiar habits. Almost every man that I heard spoken to was addressed by the title of Judge, Governor, or General. Very few were of a lower grade than Colonel, and to be called Captain or Esquire would indicate a person of doubtful reputation, or at least one not entitled to much consideration. The planters residing near Savannah usually come to the city early in the morning on horseback, or in crazy one-horse chaises, and remain during the day at the Pulaski House or some other favorite place of resort.

A Georgian is seldom seen walking in the streets,

particularly during the heat of the day. If from any cause he is obliged to resort to that kind of locomotion, he will in all probability be accompanied by his "nigger," to carry his coat or hold an umbrella over his head to keep off the sun. These Southrons have a great aversion to bodily exercise. It is a popular maxim with them, that "work was intended for niggers, *not* for gentlemen."

They are constitutionally or climatically indolent, and will sit a great part of the day in a shady place, smoking, drinking mint-juleps (which are a southern concoction), discussing the price of cotton and rice, or estimating the value of their "niggers." Occasionally they will wander into the abstruse regions of politics; but if the weather is very hot, that exciting topic is avoided, on account of its liability to engender caloric and bad feelings. The subject that most interests them is the fleecy product of the cotton plant. It is cotton in the morning, cotton at noon, and cotton at night. A kind of cotton insanity appears to affect all classes. To their distempered imaginations, cotton is the pabulum that nourishes and sustains the entire North and "the rest of mankind;" cotton, the "open sesame" to wealth, power, honor, and personal and national aggrandizement; cotton, the Atlas which upholds and the lever that moves the entire world. In fact, they consider cotton the *vis vitæ*—"the one thing needful." Upon it is based the boasted power of the South, which, without it, would sink into comparative insignificance, and the inhabitants lose their prestige with foreign nations, and in point of influence *be but little above the "mudsill" Yankees at the North.* * * *

I left on the morning of the 22d instant for Macon, a growing inland town of some size, situated at the head of steamboat navigation on the Ocmulge River, and about two hundred miles distant, by railroad, from Savannah. I found here one of the finest railroad depots that I had seen since I left the North, also a good hotel, which merits "golden opinions," if it does not reap golden rewards, for its excellent bill of fare. On an eminence overlooking the town is the Georgia Female Seminary, an imposing edifice, under the direction of the Methodist Conference, which, according to their published circular, was "instituted for the purpose of giving to female education a more systematic, thorough, and extended course than is now to be obtained in our best seminaries."

The country along the railroad, between Macon and Savannah, is level and monotonous, and the scenery, for the most part, tame and uninteresting. We passed through immense "pine barrens," with occasional patches of verdure, and innumerable swamps of tangled wild-wood, with here and there a tall, melancholy cypress, with its trailing garments of moss, looking the very impersonation of gloom. The soil, as far as I could judge, was mostly sand and a red clay, and the principal productions corn, cotton, and tobacco, with occasional fields of rice wherever the land could be overflowed. We passed numerous gangs of slaves at work on the road, or going from one plantation to another with their tools in their hands; and they would invariably "lay down the shovel and the hoe," strike an attitude, and with a comical grin gaze at the retreating cars until they were out of sight.

I spent the next night at Columbus, a staid, sober, puritanical looking town, where many of the streets were so wide and covered with verdure that they looked more like longitudinal parks than highways for travel. Some of the streets are said to be nearly two hundred feet in width, and the buildings set so far back that the place has more the appearance of a thickly settled rural district than of a city of some ten thousand inhabitants. It is situated on the Chattahoochee River, which is, at this point, the dividing line between Georgia and Alabama, and is said to have the finest water-power in the state. I remained there but one night, and had no opportunity to see much of the city, my observations being confined to a few of the streets near the principal hotel. I learned, on inquiry, that most of the business was transacted in the vicinity of the river, where there are a number of mills, manufactories, and foundries in successful operation.

A short distance above Columbus are some picturesque rapids in the Chattahoochee, overlooked by a fine rocky bluff, famous in story as the "Lover's Leap."* The flow of the river is rapid and wild, broken by rocks, over which the water frets and foams in angry surges. On each side are lofty and irregular

* The following account is condensed from the narrative of T. A. Richards, published by the Appletons.

cliffs, covered to their verge with majestic forest trees. Near here are the Falls of Coweta.

In the early part of the present century, this region was inhabited by two powerful tribes of Indians—the Cussetas and the Cowetas. Formerly they were friends, but then the bitterest of enemies. It is not related how this animosity originated, or how long it had existed; but it had rankled and burned in their breasts until its pent-up fury was ready to break out at any fancied insult or trivial cause.

The proud chief of the Cussetas had now become an old man, and was loved and venerated by all who rallied at his battle-cry. The boldest heart in all his tribe quailed before his angry eye, and the proudest did him reverence. The old man had outlived all his sons. One by one they had been called by the Great Spirit from their hunting grounds, and in the flush of their manhood had gone to the spirit-land. Yet he was not alone. The youngest of his children, the dark-eyed Mohina, was still sheltered in his bosom, and all his love for the beautiful in life was bestowed upon her. The young maiden rivalled in grace the bounding fawn, and the young warriors said of her, that " the smile of the Great Spirit was not so beautiful." While yet a child, she had been betrothed to the Young Eagle of the Cowetas, the proud scion of their warrior chief. But stern hatred had stifled kindly feelings in the hearts of all save these two young creatures, and the pledged word was broken when the smoke of the calumet was extinguished. Mohina no longer dared to meet the young chief openly, and death faced them when they sat in their lone, wild trysting-place. Their young hearts had hopes in the future, but all in vain, for time served but to render more fierce and deadly the hatred which existed between the tribes. Skirmishes were frequent between the hunters, and open hostilities seemed inevitable.

At length a jealous rival of the young Coweta tracked the maiden to the place of meeting, and peering through the tangled underwood, saw her in the arms of her lover, and heard from his lips "sweet words and passionate." He sped back to the Cussetas, gathered together their warriors, and hastened to the wild glen where the lovers were secreted. They fled on the approach of their enemies, and love and terror added wings to their flight. For a while they outran their pursuers; but the strength of Mohina failed her in a perilous moment, and had not the Young Eagle caught her to his fast beating heart, the enemy would have made sure their fate. He rushed onward up the narrow defile before him, and in a few moments stood on the verge of a dizzy, fearful height. Wildly the maiden clung to him, and even then, at that critical moment, his heart throbbed proudly beneath his burden. Already he heard the deep, labored breathing of one of his pursuers—the hated rival; and, as he slightly turned his head, the gleam of an uplifted tomahawk flashed upon his eye. The young chief gave him one quick, piercing look, and with a loud yell of triumph sprang into the seething waters below. Still the young maiden clung to him, nor yet did the death-struggle part them. The mad waves dashed fearfully over them, and their loud wail was a fitting requiem to their departing spirits. The horror-stricken warriors gazed wildly into the foaming torrent, then dashed with reckless haste down the declivity to bear the sad tidings to the old chief. He heard their tale in silence; but sorrow was on his spirit, and it was broken. Henceforth his seat was vacant by the council fire, and its red light gleamed fitfully upon his grave. * * *

After leaving Columbus we crossed the Chattahoochee River into Alabama, and proceeded by rail to this city, which is the capital of this state, and next in commercial importance to Mobile. When we entered Alabama, the appearance of the country began to improve. The soil was better; the agricultural districts richer; the scenery more varied; and all kinds of vegetation further advanced. Swelling hills crowned with trees in full foliage, and rich valleys and fertile plains clad in living verdure, with tiny streams meandering in the distance, formed a picture on which the eye delighted to linger.

I arrived in this city late in the afternoon, and secured a room at one of the best hotels, although it does not compare favorably with our third-rate New York hotels, and is not such as a stranger would expect to find in a town as large as this, and of equal commercial and political importance. I shall remain here for several days, and will write again before I take my departure. * * *

LETTER XVI.

MONTGOMERY, *April*, 1856.

THERE is a dreamy languor in the climate of the South, which indisposes one to exertion, and even the effort of letter writing—which, under ordinary circumstances, is but "a labor of love"—appears to me, at this time, to be an almost herculean task.

Montgomery is located at the head of steamboat navigation on the Alabama River, three hundred and thirty-one miles from Mobile, and has a population of about ten thousand. It is the western terminus of the Montgomery and West Point railroad, and has water communication with several important places. Its commerce is based mainly upon corn and cotton, about one hundred thousand bales of the fleecy product being annually shipped at this place. In the way of manufactures, Montgomery does but little, except, as some one has said, "to manufacture the politics of the State." It is the great political centre of the Gulf States, and the congregating place for southern politicians, newspaper reporters, office-seekers, *et hoc genus omne.*

The city is beautifully situated. The business portion is in a valley extending nearly to the river; while the capitol occupies an eminence overlooking the lower part of the city, and the country which lies beyond it. Encircling this valley is a succession of hills and gentle undulations, forming as it were a natural amphitheatre dotted with villas and country-seats. I made the circuit on horseback. Every eminence that I ascended, revealed some new object to admire; some Italian villa or cottage *orné* peeping out from its wilderness of shrubbery, or a lordly mansion reposing in dignity beneath the perennial shade of giant live-oaks—the acknowledged monarchs of the southern forests. I rode for several hours through these delightfully picturesque suburbs, and had my admiration excited at every step. Nature created this a paradise. Art adorned and beautified it. But in this flowery Eden the trail of the serpent is visible.

Notwithstanding its elevated location, the city is said to be quite unhealthy. The yellow fever, that pestilential scourge of the South, prevails here at times to an alarming extent, and other diseases less virulent in their nature seem to be, as it were, indigenous to this locality.

During my rambles I came to a spot of such quiet beauty and loveliness, that I stopped and gazed upon it for a long time in silent admiration. It was an inclosure of two or three acres, on whose swelling bosom of velvet softness reposed a modest little cottage almost buried in a wilderness of foliage and flowers. Standing near were two parental oaks, the protecting deities of the place, whose gigantic, outstretched limbs, gnarled and defiant, strove in vain to meet above, and hide their offspring from the face of the over-arching sky. Encircling this classic retreat was a perennial hedge almost smothered in the embrace of creeping vines and plants in full bloom. Roses of various hues, and the fragrant honeysuckle and yellow flowering jasmine, were intermingled, yielding alike their perfume to the breeze, and filling the surrounding air with the purest life.

A Fast City.

"A sweeter spot on earth was never found :
I looked and looked, and still with new delight,
Such joy my soul, such pleasures filled my sight."

Time flew on angels' wings, and the shades of evening were fast gathering, before I became conscious of the lateness of the hour. Returning to the hotel, I supped, and then wandered in the streets, which were as brilliant as handsome ladies and gas could make them. The shops and stores are all of modern style, and apparently well stocked with fashionable goods. Progress is unmistakably written on everything. Fogyism, that ancient enemy of enterprise and improvement, had fled at the first scream of the steam-whistle, and has not been seen here since. It is evidently a fast city, with its fast horses, fast men, and fast women. The latter are said to be the best in a long race, and generally manage to distance all their competitors. I find that two-forty is the standard time here among bipeds as well as quadrupeds, and those of less speed are excluded from the course by the arbiters of fashion.

The celebrated violinist Ole Bull gave a concert

here the other evening, assisted, according to the bills, " by an eminent pianist, a celebrated performer on the cornet, and a distinguished Prima Donna." The latter title was evidently a misnomer; as the lady, in my opinion, was not sufficiently skilled in the art of melody to be entitled to the first place in any opera, unless an Ethiopian burlesque.

Ole himself is in a very good state of preservation, considering that his life has been one of disappointments, reverses, and vicissitudes. He is not likely to hang up his fiddle and his bow for some years to come, unless so ordered by Providence; although I observed that the frosty fingers of Time had been playing with his locks and left their indelible impress.

Montgomery has more the air and appearance of a New York town than any Southern city that I have yet visited. Notwithstanding its Northern aspect, most of the inhabitants are ultra Southerners, who adhere with tenacity to their "peculiar institutions." The legislature not being in session, I have not had an opportunity to see much of the office-holding and office-seeking chivalry. Many of the guests of our hotel appear to be members of the legal profession;

at least, so I judged from their attachment to the *bar-room*, which is the best patronized part of the house. Its patrons, however, do not all seem to be professional men; but planters, cotton-brokers, and others without any particular business or occupation. The topic most frequently discussed is cotton, and "niggers," which being rather a dry subject, those engaged in it were often obliged to resort to the bar, to lubricate their vocal organs, so that they may be understood by those around them.

Montgomery has become a great mart for cotton. Nearly all that is grown in Central Alabama is brought to this city to be shipped down the river, which flows for more than four hundred miles through the richest cotton region of the South, and carries each year thousands of bales of this valuable commodity to Mobile and New Orleans. Cotton is in reality the circulating blood which gives vitality to the state. All classes are interested in its culture, from the princely merchant to the lowly artisan; the wealthy planter with his broad fields and army of slaves, as well as the humble occupant of a cabin with a few contiguous acres. A failure of the cotton crop would cast a gloom over the entire community. It would paralyze their internal commerce, create a panic in their monetary affairs, and be absolutely ruinous to all planters of small means. Negroes, unlike their masters, are never affected by the price of cotton. Sometimes their market value is slightly diminished by a failure of the crop, or increased somewhat by an abundant harvest; yet they, as a class, are generally indifferent to its fluctuations. If they are not over-tasked or abused, and have a sufficiency of creature comforts, they appear to be satisfied and happy.

I find that the cost of living at the South, especially in cities and large towns, is considerably greater than at the North. I was told by a wealthy resident of this city that it would be cheaper for him to board with his entire family—some eight or ten in number—at any of the first-class hotels in New York, than to keep house here, notwithstanding he owned all his family servants and the dwelling he occupied. Most kinds of food, with the exception of those Southern *staples*, "hog and hominy," are very dear, and the supply is not always equal to the demand. At least

I have found it so in several cases when my appetite has been sharpened by travel. Many of their luxuries are brought from the North, but frequently, when they reach their place of destination, they no longer deserve the name, time and the climate having so impaired their edible qualities as to render them only fit to be used in the manufacture of bacon.

The keeping of so many slaves about their dwellings is an important item in the expense of living. Not that the food they eat and the clothes they wear, cost so very much; but they are idle, careless, and destructive, and wasteful to excess. In the culinary department, every article of food, whether prepared or in a crude state, has to be kept under lock and key; and when wanted for use, weighed or measured out, or it will be wasted or dispensed with ruinous prodigality. I have observed, in passing some of their first-class residences, the yard literally swarming with these human chattels; frequently a dozen or more in sight, of both sexes, and comprising at least three generations. Of that number, perhaps not more than two or three were of any service to their owner; the rest being incapacitated for work, by youth, infirmity, or age. I have no doubt that two or three domestics of the Teutonic or Celtic race, at a cost of as many hundred dollars per annum, will do more work, and with much less waste, than a whole family of slaves, whose yearly keeping and *wasting* cannot be accounted less than from eight to twelve hundred dollars.

Slave labor undoubtedly is profitable to the owners or occupants of large inland plantations, away from cities and towns, where the able-bodied of both sexes are made available as field hands. But here, as well as in other populous places at the South, where they are mainly employed as house servants, or in taking care of the premises of their owners, the labor of the few hardly compensates for the cost of maintaining the many. This class of servants are allowed more liberties than plantation negroes; of these they take advantage, and shirk labor whenever they can.

To a Northerner imbued with republican principles and inheriting the sentiments and prejudices of his Puritan ancestors, the existence of slavery, in its most favorable form, must appear unnatural and forbidding. But a few months' residence at the South will, I opine, so change his views and soften his prejudices that he will regard the system with less abhorrence. I am no friend to slavery in the abstract, neither do I admire the practical workings of the system, as it is not in accordance with my views of equal-rights and universal freedom. Yet from observations made during a two months' residence at the South, I am convinced that the slaves, as a class, are not so badly off as many of us suppose. They are generally well treated, and enjoy as many, if not more physical comforts than a majority of the free negroes at the North; and I am inclined to believe that *the masters are, on the whole, more to be pitied than the slaves themselves.*

The laws of Cuba are more favorable to emancipation, and protect the negro far better than do ours. The slaves on that island, according to the Code, must be worked only a specified number of hours each day, and their masters are obliged to provide them with a permanent subsistence. On Sundays and holidays they are allowed to work in their own gardens, or employ their time as they choose. Being by law protected in the enjoyment of a certain amount of property, they can, if disposed, apply their earnings to the purchase of their own freedom. The value of a slave, which is established by arbitration, in no case exceeds five hundred dollars, although his market value may be considerably more; and as soon as he has accumulated fifty dollars, his master is obliged to accept it towards the purchase of his freedom. Every instalment thus made secures for the slave a proportionate control of his own time, and it is not uncommon to see slaves who have three or four days in the week at their disposal. In case he should be sold before the expiration of his bondage, the amount he has paid must be carried to his credit by the new owner. A slave may also have the benefit of a change of masters provided he can show that he has been ill used. If, however, he can find some one willing to become his purchaser, and the parties cannot agree upon his value, they go before a commissioner appointed by government, who fixes a price, which the owner is obliged to accept, and in return make out a bill of sale to the new purchaser. The negro may have so bad a reputation that he cannot find any one willing to buy him. In that event, he remains with his master, who having taken him for *worse* instead of *better*, as the ladies sometimes take their husbands, is obliged to feed, clothe, and take care of him during sickness and health, in decrepitude and age. But the slaves in Cuba are regarded by their owners more as chattels than human beings, and there exists none of that affectionate regard so often manifested between master and servant in the Southern States. The slaves here, as a class, are more contented and happy, and apparently much better off than most of the emancipated negroes. The free negroes of the South, to speak paradoxically, are not in reality as free as the slaves themselves, and are apparently less happy and contented. Even the African in his bondage feels his own superiority, and looks the very picture of contemptuous pity as he exclaims—" He, poor miserable nigger, has no massa to take care of him."

Among the many objectionable features in the institution of slavery, the separation of families and the sundering of conjugal ties have always appeared to me the most odious and inhuman. I find, on inquiry, that this is seldom practised—at least, not to very great extent; and from the slaves themselves,

I learn that this separation, when it does exist, is not generally regarded by them as a very great affliction.

I had a conversation a few days ago with an unctuous specimen of *Ham*-anity by the name of "Nick," who was as black as his Satanic namesake, but of fewer evil propensities, if there is any truth in physiognomy. I asked him his age.

"Thirty seben nighabouts, Massa!" said he, respectfully touching his hat.

"Are you married, Nick?"

"Yas, Massa, I spose I is!"

"How many children have you?"

"Wall, I spects I'm de fader of ten, yaw, yaw." Here he displayed a set of teeth that would have excited the envy of many a Northern belle.

"Ten children? Why, Nick, that is quite a family for so young a man as you!"

"Why yas, Massa, Ise some on children!"

"How old is your wife?"

"Do-no zackly, but reckon she be some younger dan me!"

"Is she stout and healthy?"

"She be all dat, massa!"

" Does she belong to your master?"

" No, her massa lives a heap ways from here!"

" How often do you go to see her?"

" Do-no zackly, sometimes once a month, and sometimes nary as often!"

" Wouldn't you like to see your wife and children more frequently?"

" I do-no, sar, sometimes I tink I would, but massa says I go dare nuff, and he knows better dan me."

This conversation occurred nearly as I have related it, and is a fair specimen of the stolidity and indifference of the negroes on most of the Southern plantations. I refer to the genuine, full-blooded African, before his admixture with the gentle blood of the chivalric South, for, to use a sporting phrase, "blood will tell," whether it be in the horses of the North, or in the colored chattels of the South. It is something that will reveal itself whether in man or beast. But a truce to this nonsense, this dark rendering of a *dark* subject.

I came to this city contemplating a trip down the Alabama River to Mobile, and from there to New Orleans, but the weather is becoming so hot that I almost fear, in my present state of health, to risk a visit to those "infected districts," or to trust myself for three or four days on a crowded steamer, with indifferent accommodations. If I abandon this trip, I shall seek a more invigorating climate. My next letter will probably be from New Orleans or Nashville. * * * * * * *

LETTER XVII.

NASHVILLE, TENN., May, 1856.

My last letter was written from Montgomery, that lovely city in the green heart of Alabama, where I spent a few days very pleasantly. My route from there lay in an easterly direction, for nearly a hundred miles, to the Chattahoochee River, and being diversified by hill and dale, woodland and stream, was highly picturesque. I was surprised to see so many varieties of trees, shrubs, and creeping vines in the forests and swamps through which we passed. There was the stately live-oak, the melancholy elm, the mournful cypress, the green-leaved laurel, the white-canopied dog-wood, and the scarlet-flowering red-wood, with its leafless branches thickly covered with delicate rose-tinted flowers. Conspicuous among the shrubs and vines was the wild honeysuckle with its odorous breath, and the yellow-flowering jasmine overburdened with fragrance and wreathing with graceful festoons the stately oak and lonely shrub.

After we crossed the Chattahoochee into Georgia, the country appeared less highly cultivated, and the face of Nature less attractive. The same change was visible in the faces of the inhabitants along our route, showing that animate as well as inanimate Nature is impressible and assimilating in its character, and, like the chameleon, "assumes the hue of the object with which it comes in contact." Our train proceeded quite slowly, and stopped long enough at every station to enable me to see something of the country and the inhabitants; and I must say that I was not favorably impressed with the fertility of the one or the prosperity and enterprise of the other. The land was evidently not more than half cultivated, and the buildings were rude and primitive in appearance—unlike most of our comfortable farm-houses at the North.

Cotton, rice, and sweet potatoes are the principal staples of Georgia; although the small farms in the interior produce pigs and poultry, Indian corn and tobacco, with a few kinds of grain for home consumption. The most valuable "domestic animals" are alligators, negroes, rattlesnakes, pickaninnies, and scorpions, which are indigenous to this climate, and grow spontaneously in the numerous lagoons, swamps, and rivers. But I am far from wishing to disparage this state, which is, without doubt, one of the most wealthy and enterprising of the cotton states. With a diversity of soil, and a climate half tropical, Georgia has within itself abundant sources of prosperity and wealth. Its extensive domains are traversed by navigable rivers, and its eighty miles of sea-coast are lined with islands, fertile in sea-island cotton, and capable of producing many tropical fruits and vegetables. The southern part is low, level, and interspersed with swamps, which are well adapted to the cultivation of rice. In the interior are rich alluvial bottoms and table-lands, suited to the growth of the different kinds of cotton; while many parts of the north, though mountainous and apparently almost sterile, will, if properly cultivated, yield a fair compensation to the husbandman.

I evidently passed through the most unattractive portion of the state; for I saw nothing in inanimate nature to admire, although I was greatly amused at some of the *animate* objects which came under my observation. The inhabitants, as a class, were certainly the most unpolished specimens of humanity that I ever met. But, without doubt, many of these rough back-woods-men were "the bone and sinew" of our country; men of strong hands and warm hearts, and worthy of our highest respect.

During this excursion, I saw for the first time a genuine specimen of the "Georgia cracker," fresh from the pine barrens of his native state; so that this embodiment of the spirit of youthful romance and imagination is no longer a myth, but a creature of flesh and blood—a veritable history, in which he is chronicled as the only being on *airth* capable of "administering consolation" to a live Yankee, or cute enough to out-wooden-nutmeg an itinerant Connecticut clock-pedler. He entered the cars at a small way-station near the town of La Grange, carrying on his arm a pair of old-fashioned russet-leather saddle-bags (large enough to have contained a week's provender for man and beast), which he hung on the back of an unoccupied seat, and seated himself with his face towards me, as if to give me a better opportunity to study his *physique*. In person he was tall, lean, and lantern-jawed, having what might be termed "a vegetable countenance," with *carroty* hair, *radish* cheeks, and a *turn-up* nose. He was dressed in a bran-new suit of linsey-woolsey, with a hat considerably the worse for wear, which had once evidently been black, but was now pretty nearly *dun*. One side of his face appeared to be swollen, the cause of which was soon revealed; his huge nether-jaw relaxed, his mouth opened, and a large quid of tobacco was dropped on the floor, where it remained a steaming mass of juice-extracted vegetation—an oasis in the desert waste surrounding it. Then his deep pockets were fathomed, and a huge plug of "Virginia pig-tail" was inserted between his capacious jaws. After considerable twisting and wrenching, accompanied by mirth-moving contortions of countenance, he succeeded in sundering a fragment, which he "rolled as a sweet morsel under his tongue." Turning partly around and elevating his feet, he sat for some time quietly chewing his cud, but soon changed his position, and began to exhibit unmistakable symptoms of uneasiness. He kept hitching up his trowsers, moving about in his seat, and looked the very picture of "Impatience sitting on a hemlock board and chewing the bitter cud of discontent." His eyes wandered from one person to another, as if there were something on his mind—something that he wished to say. My sympathies became excited, and I was about to address him, when he "broke the ice," and let in upon us a stream of volubility almost overwhelming. Being the nearest to him, I had to brave the force of the deluge; I shuddered at each successive douche, but was compelled to let the torrent flow on, without making any effort to check its impetuosity, merely endeavoring to divert it into some other channel.

I have a great dislike to talking in the cars, when they are in motion, as the effort to raise my voice above the din and noise of the rattling train seriously affects my throat; but there was no way of dodging the tongue-missiles of this loquacious individual. If he had talked without requiring an answer, I would not have cared; but he opened the conversation, as you would an oyster, by the introduction of the inquisitorial knife. Listen to him for a moment:

"Wal, stranger, this ere's dusty trav'ling!"

"Yes," I replied.

"You don't live in these ere parts, I reckon?"

"No!"

"Whar' may you be from?"

"Cuba."

"What! that are island of Cuby! How's the cotton crop down thar'?"

"I believe that cotton is not one of the products of that island," I replied.

"What! not raise cotton? Make shingles I spose!"

"No, I think not!"

"Lots of niggers thar' I dare say! and plenty of tobaccy tew! How many niggers dew yew own?"

"I am not the owner of any."

"Wal! that's curious, not to own no niggers! perhaps you hires 'em, dew yew?"

Being anxious to change the conversation, which was becoming almost too familiar, I did not heed his last remark, but inquired what business he was engaged in. Stretching his long, ostrich-like neck over the side of the seat, he ejected from his mouth a superfluous quantity of tobacco juice; then leaning over towards me, in a sort of half-confiding tone replied, " Wal! Mister, I'm in the shingle business, I am. Now there is lots of ways of gettin' a livin' in this ere world; some folks by keepin' niggers and raisin' cotton; some by sellin' traps and swappin' hosses; some by lumberin' and farmin'. Now you see I've had a smart chance at most of these businesses, besides tendin' saw-mill and boatin', but this ere shingle business beats 'em all."

"But," said I, " do you find this business profitable?"

"Wal, not particularly so, but I kinder manage to get enough grub for the old woman and children, and that's about all we orter expect in this ere world."

"How large a family have you?" I asked.

"Wal, let's see, there's the old woman and four gals and tew boys to home, besides Joe and Silas who's away down the 'Hooche a lumberin'."

How much longer he would have edified me with his cracker jargon I am unable to say, had he not, on turning his head to expectorate, caught sight of an acquaintance in the forward part of the car. Making his way in that direction he grasped the man by the hand, and exclaimed in a voice loud enough to be heard by all around him:—

"How do yu dew, Square? I'm mitey glad tu see yu; been down to the plantation I reckon? Wal, I *de*-clare if this ere aint Molly as I live! How she's growed! I say, Square, this ere's a smart gall of yourn, and looks on-commonly like her ma."

He continued to hold forth in this strain until he arrived at his place of debarkation; when throwing his saddle-bags over his shoulder, and shaking his friend's hand, he exclaimed:

"Now, Square, when yu come down tu our district, come rite to my cabin, plenty of hog and hominy, and the old woman will be mitey glad tu see yu."

This picture is drawn from life, and those who know the original will acknowledge the correctness of the delineation.

About sunset we reached Atlanta, a town of some importance from its being a market and place of transhipment for most of the cotton and other articles of export, raised in several of the adjoining counties. Two or three railroads intersect there, which makes it a place of considerable bustle and activity. I was recommended by a gentleman on the cars to the "Trout House," which favorably impressed me with its appetizing name. It proved to be a large unpainted brick building, four stories high, and of not very prepossessing exterior. The interior was cold, cheerless, and inhospitable, and I began to think that its name was its only attraction. The porter who took charge of my luggage was evidently the *major-domo* of the establishment, for he was the only person visible while I was engaged in registering my name and selecting a room for the night.

Calling for a glass of iced-water, I was told that there was none in the house, but if I would pay for it, they would send out and get some for me. I thought this was rather cool treatment, but supposing it to be one of the customs of the country, I gave the porter a quarter, and in about an hour a small pitcher of ice, but no change, was brought to my room in the fourth story.

This world, or the inhabitants thereof, are said to be composed of two antagonistic classes—"victims and victimizers." I certainly shall be at no loss hereafter to decide to which class *I* belong. But, as

Hudibras says there is as "great pleasure in being cheated as to cheat," I shall have my full share of this world's pleasures and beatitudes.

When I came down to tea, the table was nearly deserted; but from the soiled condition of the cloth, and the refuse eatables scattered around, I judged that quite a number of hungry bipeds had preceded me. When seated, a full-blooded African, with a face as black as the ace of spades, and a mouth stretching from ear to ear, came up and wanted to know "what massa would be helped to." Before I could reply, a spruce-looking mulatto, who evidently imagined that he saw a shining quarter in the perspective, approached me and bowing very obsequiously, said, "I will take the gentleman's order!"

"No, you doant," said he with the open countenance, "I'm gwine to wait on de gemman myself," and he reached out his hand to take my plate. I ended the controversy by waving off the interloper, and directed the sable individual to bring me a plate of dry toast with a cup of black tea.

"Yaw! yaw! dat I will, massa!" and he started for the kitchen as fast as his lagging heels would allow him, those elongated appendages not being able to keep within two or three feet of his advancing head and shoulders. He returned in a few moments almost out of breath, the perspiration standing in large drops on his ebony forehead, from his efforts to toast my bread over a hot coal-fire. His first salutation was:

"Dat are free nigger 'magines I don't know how to wait on the white folks. Him feels mitey grand since he got free papers! But I'll let him know dat he's no better dan me no how." He wiped his face with his coat-sleeve, and in his anxiety to please, placed before me pepper, mustard, salt, and other condiments which I did not require, and neglected to pass the butter, and the necessary ingredients for my tea. When I asked for the latter, he upset the sugar-bowl in his haste to reach it, and filled my cup to overflowing with milk before I could prevent it. At last I was obliged to send him to the kitchen for something I did not want, to get rid of his well meaning but awkward attempts to serve me.

On examining the edibles before me, I found that my heedless waiter had mistaken my order, and instead of dry toast and black tea, had brought me *black* toast and *dry* tea, for the one was black as Sambo himself, and the other tasted more like a decoction of dried herbs than of savory oolong. But finding a plate of stale bread within my reach, I made a hasty though not luxurious meal—being desirous to get away from the table before the return of my officious waiter.

Not finding any late papers in the hotel, or anything to interest me within doors, I strolled through some of the principal streets in the vicinity; observed nothing worthy of note, but enough, however, to convince me that Atlanta was the most unattractive place that I had seen since leaving Cuba. About nine o'clock " a solitary wayfarer"—to use the language of a popular novelist, " might have been seen wending his weary way" up three flights of stairs to his quiet room in the "upper regions." Here he remained in close communion with Morpheus until the first train left in the morning, when he took his departure, having acquired, during his brief sojourn, a little more knowledge of Southern manners and customs.

My next stopping-place was Chattanooga, a small inland town within the limits of Tennessee, where I remained one night and the greater part of a day; from necessity, however, not from choice, as the cars were detained there that length of time. The passengers were quite indignant at the apparently unnecessary delay. It was intimated that the railroad company had a pecuniary interest in the badly-kept hotel at the station; otherwise a score or two of impatient travellers would not be so often delayed there, and subjected to such poor fare and indifferent accommodations. I would rather have spent the night on a *rail* than in a seven-by-nine room, on a bed of straw, between sheets *not* as immaculate as the driven snow. But I passed the ordeal unscathed, and reached this city in safety. While at Chattanooga, I was obliged to remain in the hotel most of the time, on account of a severe rain storm, and as there were no books or papers accessible, I amused myself with watching the crowd of "natives" who thronged the bar-room, and in listening to their ludicrous provincialisms. They would come in wet as drowned rats, but immediately complain of being *dry*, and forthwith proceed to "imbibe." The smiling proprietor stood behind the counter in his shirt sleeves, engaged in preparing a suspicious combination of fluid commodities with "mint fixings," and dispensing it with alacrity to the thirsty crowd who were impatiently awaiting their turn at "the straw," which they sucked with apparent relish. It has been said that "straws show which way the wind blows," but in this instance they plainly indicated *the way the streams flowed*. * * *

Nashville, the capital of Tennessee, is pleasantly situated on the Cumberland River, and has a population of about twenty-five thousand. This stream rises in the south-eastern part of Kentucky, and after making a bend into this State, and pursuing its elliptical course for nearly two hundred miles, it runs north, into western Kentucky, and empties into the Ohio River, a short distance from its confluence with "the Father of Waters." The chief attraction of this city is its picturesque and commanding situation, and the beauty and diversity of the surrounding scenery. It is mostly built upon a solid rock a hundred feet or more above the bed of the river, and, on account of its elevated and healthful location, has become a popular resort during the summer, for families living in the low and less salubrious places in the vicinity.

Nashville contains many fine private residences, but the "lion" of the city, as well as of the state, is the elegant capitol now in process of erection. It is built of Tennessee marble, a species of limestone susceptible of a beautiful polish, which was found in that vicinity. The expense of this structure, when completed, will be not far from one million of dollars, notwithstanding the first cost of the stone was but nominal, and it was quarried and worked by convicts from the State Prison. It stands upon the highest eminence in the city, nearly two hundred feet above the river, and is a conspicuous mark for the eye for leagues around. This edifice was designed by a Philadelphia architect named Strickland, who died about two years ago, and by a special permit his remains were entombed in a vault beneath the building. His son, also an architect, is now engaged in completing the work. In one of the pleasantest streets of the city is the mansion of the late President Polk, where his widow now resides. On the lawn in front of the house is a monument erected by Mrs. Polk to the memory of her statesman-husband, containing a simple and appropriate inscription.

This city is celebrated for its beautiful women, but as I only had an opportunity to see them in church and in their carriages, at a distance, I cannot speak intelligently on the subject; for distance is supposed to "lend enchantment" to animate as well as inanimate objects. I was much pleased with the bright happy faces of a cavalcade of school-girls, who passed me one day in the outskirts of the city. They were all quite pretty, becomingly attired, and rode with ease and elegance.

The country, for leagues around Nashville, is picturesque and beautiful, pleasantly diversified with hill and dale, with cultivated fields, green pastures, and belts of woodland. It is an opulent district, highly cultivated, and abounding in extensive plantations, with fine old mansions, where the wealthy planters live more like noblemen than simple farmers.

The inhabitants of the South, particularly the planters of affluence, are celebrated for their hospitality and courtesy to strangers. It is a part of their religion "to take in strangers," and entertain them at their homes and firesides. Any one having just claims to respectability is cordially welcomed by them, and horses, carriages, and servants are placed at his command. He is invited to join in all the social gatherings in the neighborhood, and is expected to make himself at home in every sense of the word. This is a charming feature of Southern society, and an agreeable contrast to the ungenial and indifferent manner with which strangers are often treated at the North. It is true, that strangers, with us, are " taken in," but not always in the scriptural sense; neither are they often the recipients of that genuine, unselfish hospitality which is so universal among the planters and wealthy citizens of the South. I speak somewhat from experience, having in several instances, during my southern travels, received civilities and personal attentions such as would not have been bestowed on a stranger at the North. * * *

LETTER XVIII.

"MAMMOTH CAVE HOTEL,"* KY., *May*, 1856.

THE long cherished desire of my life is realized. I have seen the Mammoth Cave, the *eighth* wonder of the world, and by many considered more wonderful than all the others combined. I have traversed its majestic avenues, threaded its tortuous paths, climbed its precipitous heights, peered into its Tartarean depths, navigated its Stygian waters, drunk from its Crystal fountains, ascended its Rocky Mountains, and gazed on its varied scenes with conflicting emotions. I was awed by its grandeur, charmed by its sublimity, fascinated by its beauty, and astonished at its immensity.

* Some portions of the following letter were published in a newspaper at the time when it was written. In its revised and enlarged form, as here presented, the author hopes that he has succeeded in depicting the most striking features of the Mammoth Cave.

But to particulars. I left Nashville in company with a Mr. L., from New York, an elderly gentleman of wealth and education, whose acquaintance I made in Havana. We reached "Bell's Tavern" the next night, by stage. This has been "a place of entertainment for man and beast" for more than fifty years, and is intimately associated with the Mammoth Cave, being but about eight miles distant from it. Having partaken of an early breakfast the next morning, we started for the cave in an old-fashioned Kentucky "carry-all" without springs, and after riding for two hours over the worst road imaginable, reached our place of destination, pretty effectually shaken up. We were the only passengers for the cave, it being too early in the season for a great influx of visitors.

The "Cave Hotel" is a large, irregular, rambling sort of building, somewhat out of repair, and not particularly attractive in its appearance, but workmen are engaged in rejuvenating it for the coming season, when it will appear in its new annual suit of paint and garniture. The proprietor being absent when we arrived, we were obliged to wait his return before we could obtain rooms, and in the interval made the acquaintance of a young Scotchman named Frazer, who had arrived a few hours before us, and was waiting for an opportunity to join some party going into the cave. We found him an agreeable, well informed young man, and apparently familiar with most of the great natural curiosities of Europe. He had come to this country to see some of our celebrities, more especially to visit the Mammoth Cave, whose fame, it appears, is even greater in the *Old* World than in the *New*.

I am informed that the original owner of the cave, or rather of a few acres surrounding the entrance, went abroad without having explored it. While in Europe, so much interest was manifested in this wonderful natural curiosity, and he heard such extravagant accounts from persons who had visited it, that immediately on his return he purchased seventeen hundred acres more, supposing that it would cover the whole extent of the cave. But from recent explorations, it is evident that it extends under many of the farms in the vicinity, whose owners may not be aware that the Nobility of Europe, as well as the *noble men* of America, have traversed their domains "without leave or license."

This cave is said to contain "two hundred and twenty-six avenues, forty-seven domes, eight cataracts, twenty-three pits, besides numerous rivers;" the aggregate length of all the different avenues, both direct and lateral, is estimated at *three hundred miles.* It is, in fact, a small subterranean state of itself, which might almost claim to be admitted separately into the Union, if it had any population save "rats, bats, and eyeless fish," to legislate and enjoy the rights of suffrage. I am not sure, however, but it can take care of itself, having done so from time immemorial, which is more than *all* states can say! And I think I can show that the legislative, executive, and judiciary departments of this embryo state can be filled from among its own population. What is more necessary to successful legislation, than age, experience, wisdom, and sagacity? "As *old* as a rat," showing that they have age; "As *wise* as a rat," proving that they possess wisdom; and "as *cunning* as a rat," evincing their sagacity; are expressions familiar to us all. And how can the judiciary department be better filled than by eyeless fish? Slippery and supple in their natures, they can wriggle themselves deeper into the intricate interstices of the law than most of its modern disciples; and such is their affinity for shiners that they can decoy them from their clients' pockets *ad libitum*, which is one of the most important requisites in law, according to the popular interpretation of Blackstone. And besides, being *blind*, they are eminently qualified to administer justice with impartiality. As for the bats, their usefulness is manifold. They also will make successful lawyers. Being protean in their forms, they can change to suit the exigencies of the occasion, or whenever their interests demand it; and if necessary, can act as counsel to both parties in a suit, being *bird* to one, and *animal* to the other. Then again, they will make invaluable soldiers, forming in themselves a *bat*-tery that can never be silenced; and when defending a fortification, will not leave the walls during daylight, and will be occupied the entire night in flying from place to place, aiding and encouraging one another. Now I hope that our "Uncle Samuel" will give that little "bone of contention," Kansas, a toss over the Rocky

Mountains, and take into his family this underground territory with its interesting population, and I will wager a leaden ducat that the whole confederacy will be improved by the annexation. But a truce to this nonsense.

After having secured rooms, our first inquiry was for Stephen the celebrated guide, who is so closely identified with the cave and its associations, having been employed in that capacity for nineteen years. He was the first to explore many of its interminable labyrinths, and to open to the world its unrevealed wonders. We were disappointed to find that he had gone into the cave with a party early that morning, and would not be back until night. Stephen is almost as much of a celebrity as the cave itself, and I had set my heart on having him for our guide; for without his agreeable companionship, the cave to *me* would be divested of many of its attractions. But Mat, the next best guide, was not engaged, and we secured his services. About an hour was occupied in preparing lamps, changing our dresses, and other preliminaries. When completed, our party, consisting of three persons besides the guide, left the house, and after going down a winding path for about two hundred yards, reached the mouth of the cave. We were quite fantastically dressed, in "monkey jackets" of green and yellow flannel, trowsers of the same material, stuffed caps, heavy boots, a Mont Blanc staff (a long stick sharpened at the end), and each of us carrying a swinging lamp, so constructed that it could not be broken or easily extinguished. Mat carried two lamps, a canteen of oil slung on his shoulder, a basket containing our dinner, and a long black bottle, contents unknown, but *not* unsuspected. His pockets were filled with matches, Bengal lights, medicated paper, and other indispensable articles.

After descending a flight of rudely constructed stone steps for about thirty feet, we found ourselves within the mouth of the cave. Branches of trees, roots, and creeping vines overhung the entrance, imparting to it a wild and peculiarly picturesque appearance. A current of cold air greeted us as we entered, but, after advancing a few rods, we were sufficiently warm. The temperature of this cave is uniform throughout, never varying more than one degree from fifty-nine Fahrenheit, during summer or winter. The air is also remarkably pure, and so very bracing, that a person in ordinary health can walk a long distance without fatigue. Combustion is perfect in all parts of the cave, even in the deepest pits and most confined places; and it is said that nothing has ever been found here in a decomposed state. Some affirm that decomposition cannot take place where the temperature is unvarying, and the air free from humidity.

In support of this theory, it is related that Mr. Croghan, the owner of the cave, when exploring a new avenue a few years ago, discovered a young child lying on the ground apparently asleep. It was cold to the touch, yet he could hardly believe that life was extinct, so blooming were its cheeks, and so life-like the expression of its countenance. He had it removed to the hotel, and made every effort to discover its paternity, supposing that it belonged to some poor family in the vicinity. But imagine his astonishment, when visiting the body the next morning, to find nothing left but ashes. It had probably been entombed for years. * * *

Our guide having lighted the lamps and distributed

them among our party, we followed him through "The Narrows" down a gradual descent, and in a few moments emerged into the vestibule or antechamber of the cave. Most of the places of interest here are named from some incident in their history, or from the object or place to which they bear a real or imaginary resemblance. This is called the Rotunda, and is said to be one hundred and sixty feet below the surface of the earth, and nearly under the hotel.

Here our guide disappeared with the lamps, and we were plunged suddenly into darkness. The transition was so great, that it seemed as if all the sable elements were mixed together and intensified. It was horribly, awfully dark.

> "As dark as was chaos, ere the infant sun
> Was rolled together, or had tried his beams
> Athwart the gloom profound."

Soon a soft mellow light was reflected in the distance, which radiated and diffused itself over the huge grey walls above and around us. It was a scenic display, for which we were indebted to our guide and a Bengal light. We were in a room nearly two hundred feet in diameter and about sixty feet high; the roof of which is flat, and composed of a single rock, without any discernible seam or interruption, save at the edges. The whole is without a pillar or support of any kind—a wonderful triumph of the Mighty Architect and Builder.

Here are to be seen the remains of vats and furnaces used in the manufacture of saltpetre, which nearly half a century ago was taken from this cave in large quantities. Heaps of nitrous earth and ashes are scattered about, and the impression of wheels and the track of oxen are as distinctly visible as if made but a few days since.

After passing the Great Bend, where the avenue makes almost an acute angle, we came to a place designated as "The Sick Chamber." Here are to be seen two or three dilapidated stone huts, which were erected several years ago as a kind of hospital for consumptives. The pure air of the cave, and its exemption from atmospheric changes, suggested the idea of its becoming a hibernating place for pulmonic invalids, and several were induced to try the experiment. But the eternal darkness and gloom, together with the absence of enlivening society and other healthful influences, prevented a cure being effected. The last patient having persevered for more than a year without any apparent benefit, during which time two or three of his companions died, the scheme was abandoned, and the huts have remained ever since untenanted.

Two passages diverge from this mammoth chamber. One is called the Great Bat Room, from the quantities of bats to be seen upon its walls and ceiling—looking from below like black incrustations, so closely are they packed together. The other is known as the Grand Gallery; it is five miles long, from fifty to one hundred feet wide, averages about fifty feet in height, and is said to be the most extensive subterranean avenue in the known world. The next place of interest is the Church, an immense room, sixty feet high, over one hundred feet in diameter, and capable of accommodating a congregation of several thousand. A large rock projects on one side, forming an imposing pulpit, while in the rear is a niche of sufficient capacity to hold an organ and a respectable-sized choir. Divine service has been held here a number of times to large audiences. The shape and formation of this underground sanctuary are said to be in accordance with acoustic principles, and a voice of ordinary capacity will fill the room and be heard distinctly in the remotest part. Here our guide ignited a piece of medicated paper, which diffused a soft, mellow effulgence —a sort of "dim, religious light" over the room, adding to its solemnity, and leaving our minds more deeply impressed with its holy beauty and sublimity.

In contradistinction, a few hundred yards distant is the Ball Room, so called from its adaptation to the Terpsichorean art, and where the "poetry of motion" can be *perpetrated* without annoyance to the "*upper* ten thousand," who repudiate that species of amusement. It is nearly two hundred feet in diameter, and of corresponding height. A large natural orchestra projects at one end, capable of holding one hundred musicians; and the back recedes, forming a sightly gallery for spectators.

Not very far from this room is a large isolated rock standing upon the ground, called the Giant's Coffin, from its resemblance to the last tenement of humanity.

It is fifty-seven feet long, and in every way shaped like a coffin. Directly above it on the ceiling is a black incrustation of gypsum resembling an ant-eater on a log, which the superstitious consider as ominous. Back of this is a hole in the wall leading to a low room about one hundred feet square, called the Wooden Bowl, from its fancied resemblance in shape to that article of domestic utility.

We now go down "the Steeps of Time," by a rapid descent of about fifty feet, to the Deserted Chambers, a succession of gloomy-looking apartments, which are correctly named. The ground about here is full of fearful-looking chasms and pits, of which we are constantly warned by our guide. Near one of the largest of these openings, which is fearfully deep, is constantly heard the sound of an invisible waterfall.

We descended by a long ladder into the Labyrinth, so called on account of its numerous intricate passages and bewildering mazes, which we threaded in safety, although not without slightly endangering our vision, having to look to "the right and left oblique," as it were, simultaneously. Some of these passages were so irregular and complex in their structure that it would require an able mathematician to elucidate them. Its continuity of obtuse, acute, and right angles; its crooked, curved, mixed, concave, and convex lines, would puzzle a student in geometry, and convince him that there are more things *below* the earth "than are dreamt of in *his* philosophy."

The next place of interest is Goran's Dome, by many considered the greatest curiosity in the cave. Our guide led us to an opening in the wall of two or three feet in diameter, and then disappeared with our lamps. Soon a faint straggling light appeared from within this opening, which rapidly increased until the whole interior was illuminated. We each in our turn looked within. A huge yawning chasm was above and below, so high that the top was scarcely visible, so deep that the eye could not fathom it. The height and depth are estimated at three hundred feet, and the opening where we stood was about midway between the top and bottom. It is not the magnitude alone of this vast cavernous Temple, which constitutes its chief attraction; its peculiar formation, its architectural completeness, and the uniqueness of its interior decorations, are wonderful, and cannot be correctly described or delineated. The inner walls are honeycombed and covered with a creamy white incrustation. The dome above is conical in shape, and looks not unlike an immense canopy lined with richly embossed velvet (a beautiful specimen of Nature's handiwork) which descends in voluminous folds—draping the whole interior.

We retrace our steps to the Labyrinth, and continue to go down, down, down, until we stand upon the very brink of the Bottomless Pit—a frightful-looking abyss, of incredible depth. A sheet of medicated paper is lighted and thrown down, which is lost to sight long before it is extinguished; the sulphurous fumes, as they ascend, are *strongly* suggestive of—you know what!

This is two miles from the mouth of the cave, and was once supposed to be the end of all cavities in that direction. But a gentleman, a few years ago, conceived the idea that there were other openings beyond. With the aid of the adventurous Stephen, he threw a ladder over the chasm, some twenty feet, and a new field was opened for exploration. A substantial bridge is now erected here, which is crossed in perfect safety.

A short walk brings us to an opening in the ground, large enough to admit one person at a time, over which is suspended an immense rock of several tons weight, resting on a corner, looking as if the least jar would cause it to descend and close the entrance for ever. This is called the Scotchman's Trap, and is so fearful a place that many visitors, rather than enter it, will forego the pleasure of viewing the wonders which lie beyond. We go down, and soon find ourselves in the midst of huge rocks, over which we climb, long ladders which we descend, and narrow places which we squeeze through, until we come to the far-famed " Winding Way," or Fat Man's Misery, as it is facetiously termed, being a zigzag path about seven feet high, and averaging but eighteen inches in width, for a distance of three hundred and fifteen feet through a solid rock. This passage was undoubtedly formed by the gradual attrition of water, as its sides are as smooth and lustrous as a water-worn pebble.

This wonderful freak of Nature is a source of great merriment to the visitors, especially if there happen to be any *Falstaffs* among them, for it is next to impossible for a very fleshy person to get through; and several, who, with more curiosity than discretion, made the attempt, were with difficulty extricated. Some, who succeed in forcing their way through, cannot be induced to *break their fast* while on the other side, lest their *increased diameter* should prevent their safe return. My friend Mr. L———, being a small man, glided through this tortuous channel like an eel; while the great " broth of a boy" from Edinburgh, being full six feet in his stockings, and of goodly proportions, " puffed and blowed like a fresh-water porpoise," and by the time he reached a breathing-place had become longitudinally *more*, and latitudinally *less* by the severe lateral pressure. Being neither great nor small, I was fortunate enough to reach the end; but not without sundry squeezes and divers affectionate embraces from the cold unyielding walls which encompassed me. But the end was not yet. We had another ordeal to pass through, which to *me* was much more disagreeable. It was the Valley of Humility—a kind of prospective Purgatory, where the ceiling was less than four feet from the ground.

Here we were obliged to grovel in the dust, or to walk with horizontal spines, with head and back in constant danger of collision with the rough rock above. Oh, how I longed to "take off my head and carry it under my arm," like some of the personages who figure in ghost stories. It was labor to the head as well as to the back-bone, and we all uttered spontaneous exclamations of delight when we reached Relief Hall.

The next place of interest is the Bacon Chamber, where the low ceiling is covered with white oblong stalactites, being a very good imitation of hams *ready bagged and whitewashed;* and a cavity is shown in the centre, as "a kettle to boil them in." A little further on is River Hall, where the river has been known to rise fifty-seven feet above low water. We descended gradually for a long distance; the soil, a tenacious clay, is moist and slippery, the effects of a recent inundation. At the foot of this hill is a yawning abyss, known as the Dead Sea, the waters of which are said to be twenty-five feet deep at the lowest tide. A lighted paper is thrown down upon a broad, black body of water, eighty feet below—a shuddering, fearful place to look into—its Tartarean depths, its name, and the associations connected with it, all combining to impress us with sensations not easily to be shaken off. Far below us in the darkness and gloom is the river Styx. A rock is hurled into the *Erebean* space—a low, gurgling sound is heard—then all is still, and a death-like silence prevails. We prepared to descend, but our aged friend, through fear or fatigue, declined going any further, and as we could not leave him behind, we were obliged to return. I was not sorry that it so happened, for I was particularly desirous of having Stephen the Charon to ferry us over the Styx, and to hear the tones of his rich barytone voice, while passing the Echo River, on our voyage down the Lethe. We decided to return by the way of the Gothic Avenue, and to explore that portion of the cave, which would about use up the day. It was now past meridian, and having breakfasted at an unusually early hour, our stomachs began to remonstrate against so long a fast. We therefore got up an impromptu meeting, and "resolved unanimously" that it was time for dinner. Our guide spread a collation upon a rock, around which we assembled. The basket containing the mysterious bottle, with its nose provokingly in sight, as if to tempt us to a more intimate acquaintance, was placed a little distance from us, but the cold chicken was equally as tempting and much more available, *being within reach.* The three miles of locomotion, the acrobatic feats I had involuntarily performed, besides occasionally practising in " ground and lofty *tumbling,*" had given me some symptoms of fatigue, as well as an appetite; so I concluded first to try the chicken and its accompaniments, and if they failed to sustain me, then I would employ Mat as a " medium" to exorcise the *spirits* from the depths of that long, black, sepulchral-looking bottle.

Dinner being over, the fragments gathered together, the " spirits" in *their proper place,* and the empty bottle filled with surplus enthusiasm, to be uncorked when wanted, we began retracing our steps to the beginning of new wonders.

It is not my intention to give a detailed account of all the various avenues, halls, domes, and other wonders which I have seen; it would fill a volume, and exhaust my vocabulary. I shall only attempt to describe a few of the most imposing and attractive features of the Cave, which is no vast charnel-house, impure, unarchitectural, and commonplace, but a succession of splendid streets, domes, and arches, all buried deep within the earth, far from the din and strife of active life, where the lightning is never seen, thunder never heard, and the petty convulsions of nature never felt. It is an empire in ruins; a city sepulchred by mountains, its half buried palaces, halls, and domes, still revealed and visible in their full architectural beauty; its cornices, its galleries, its vaulted ceilings, " wonderfully symmetrical and mysteriously upheld." And then, the diversity of its scenery, the variety of its formations, its mountains, rivers, cataracts, its interminable labyrinths, its unfathomable abysses, its domes entombed, its palaces in ruins, all combine to make it one of the grandest, most sublime, and beautiful specimens of the handiwork of the Great Architect—Him

"——Whose breath can still the winds,
Uncloud the sun, charm down the swelling sea,
And stop the floods of Heaven."

The Gothic Avenue is two miles long, from thirty to forty feet wide, and of a corresponding height. It received its name from the curiously arched ceiling, which bears a rude resemblance to Gothic architecture. Its walls are covered with hanging stalactites, some of which are white and lustrous like Parian marble; others as clear and transparent as crystal. Many of these crystallizations depend in huge masses from the ceilings, and are of such peculiar brilliancy, that they might, at a distance, be mistaken for immense chandeliers covered with diamonds. These brilliant incrustations glittered and coruscated in the light of our uplifted torches, as we waved them to and fro beneath the gem-studded canopy.

In this vicinity, are many novel and interesting places, whose peculiar nomenclature is derived from Biography, History sacred and profane, Zoology, Mythology, and *the imagination.* I visited the Haunted Chamber, stood for a while beneath Annetti's Dome, drank from the Crystal Pool, leaned upon Napoleon's Breast-work, gathered cinders from Vulcan's Forge, saw the Elephant's Head, tweaked St. Anthony's Nose, and becoming weary, rested myself in the

Devil's arm-chair. The seat dedicated to his Satanic Majesty is a stalagmitic formation, the top of which is sufficiently depressed to afford a comfortable resting-place for the visitor. But I was so dull or unimaginative, as not to be able to discover in it any particular resemblance to an arm-chair.

The principal attraction of this avenue is the Gothic Chapel, which is of such unique formation, and so peculiar and elaborate in its ornamentation, as to excite wonder and admiration in the beholder. It is a sort of Gothic Temple, elliptical in shape, and some fifty by eighty feet in diameter. The lofty ceiling is supported by stalagmite columns, and ribbed and bracketed with stalactites. These columns expand into majestic arches as they approach the ceiling, where they unite with the stalactical drapery from above, which descends in massive folds, giving to the whole interior a grand and imposing appearance. Our guide so arranged the lights as to cause their reflections to fall upon the ceiling and the supporting columns, which so increases the effect, that the spectator can almost imagine himself to be gazing upon the interior of some vast Cathedral or Gothic

Temple of antiquity. Before leaving this avenue, we visited the Register Room, but did not leave our "handwriting on the wall," not being ambitious of that kind of immortality. The ceiling here is but ten or twelve feet high, and would be as smooth and white as plaster of Paris, were it not that many visitors, to gratify a low, morbid vanity, trace their names in vile lamp-smoke; thus blackening and disfiguring one of the most chaste and beautiful apartments in this vast Temple of Nature.

The beauty of many parts of this cave has been marred by visitors breaking off and carrying away the most beautiful stalactites and other formations, which can never be replaced. This wanton vandalism is unpardonable, from the fact, that the ground in many places is covered with beautiful specimens which have fallen from above, and may be had for the picking up. In one of the small grottoes, celebrated for the beauty of its dog-tooth spar, a few years ago, a creature wearing the semblance of humanity, broke off and carried away one of the largest and most beautiful of these crystallizations. Not content with this desecration, he inscribed his name on the fragment remaining, not omitting his undeserved title of "Reverend," for it appears that this sacrilegious despoiler of God's workmanship was *a clergyman.*

After leaving this avenue, we come to a place of peculiar interest to susceptible youths and sentimental young ladies, who are said to be on the *qui vive* when they enter its precincts. It is called "the Lover's Leap;" although I could discover nothing in the spot or its surroundings to warrant so expressive an appellative. A long, narrow, pointed rock is to be seen projecting quite a distance over a deep pit full of jagged rocks and broken stones. But I could not learn that it had ever been the scene of any such imbecile exploit as is suggested by the name. We now retraced our steps to the main avenue, and after a short respite proceeded to the Star Chamber, by far the most solemn, grand, and imposing apartment in this cave. And I can say—without partaking of any of my *bottled enthusiasm*—that I witnessed while there one of the most sublimely beautiful sights I ever beheld, and one that I shall never forget as long as memory sits securely upon her throne. This "Chamber," as it is called, is a long, magnificent hall, sixty feet high, with a flat ceiling. The walls on each side are of a light color, and are nearly perpendicular until within a few feet of the top, when they recede, making the room appear of an immense height. The ceiling is covered with a black incrustation of gypsum, studded with crystals, which have the appearance of stars in a dark night; and so perfect is the illusion, that one can hardly persuade himself that the sky is not visible through an opening in the roof. Our guide, who understands the dramatic effect to be produced by "lights and shadows," placed our lamps under a rock, so as to throw a soft, mellow light upon the ceiling, revealing the delicate marbling of the sky, and its artistically blended lights and shades. Then he would increase the shadow, to give the appearance of an approaching storm, until the whole heavens were darkened by the threatening clouds. All that was wanting to complete the illusion was the lightning's vivid flash, and the deep mutterings of the distant thunder. It was a scene that cannot well be described, but must be seen to be appreciated.

This ended our first day's exploration.—We had been six hours in darkness (except what little light was emitted from our faintly glimmering lamps), and had walked about nine miles. When we emerged from the cave, the sun was shining brightly, and we were almost blinded by the intensity of light. The air felt hot and oppressive, although the day was not very warm, and we all complained of a feeling of prostration that we did not experience in the Cave. We, however, succeeded in reaching the Hotel, and eight o'clock found *me* courting sleep with "an alacrity" worthy of Sancho Panza.

The next morning, daylight and *I* opened our eyes simultaneously; and long before Old Sol was fairly awake, the Scotchman and myself, and Stephen, with his "lamps trimmed and burning," had entered upon our three-mile journey to that subterranean river of Oblivion known as Lethe.

As our guide will figure somewhat conspicuously in this narration, a short description of him, I trust, will not be considered inappropriate, or prove uninteresting. It will at least serve to occupy the time until I see some new *natural* curiosity to describe.

Stephen is said to be an Indian-mulatto (a curious admixture truly), but he has more the physiognomy of the Spaniard than of the Indian or African. He is rather below medium size, symmetrically formed, athletic, and celebrated for his daring exploits and love of adventure. He is now about forty years of age, and, like most celebrities, has been accustomed to good society. Having associated so much with scientific men, and the *literati* of all nations, he has acquired a smattering of several different languages, and become familiar with most of the geological formations of the cave. He can discourse quite learnedly upon Geology and its kindred sciences, and will detect a piece of stalagmite from a stalactite, as readily as a skilful lapidary will distinguish a real diamond from an imitation. His features are quite refined and classical, and his countenance has a mild and pleasant expression. His complexion is of a dark olive, and his "love of a moustache," together with his black curling hair and dark melancholy eyes, are undoubtedly daguerreotyped on the heart of many a sable damsel. Having recently obtained his freedom, he has some idea of emigrating to Liberia, but his attachment to this cave and its surroundings is so great that I doubt whether he can ever be induced to be separated from it. One would suppose that he would become tired of going over the same ground day after day, and year after year, but he assured me that it was "labor of love" to him, that he seldom passed through it without discovering some new beauty, some hitherto unrevealed attraction, and that he never would tire of traversing its silent halls and solitary avenues. Stephen was very communicative, and pointed out every place of interest. He showed us where the body of a woman was found when the cave was first explored. It was in a good state of preservation, although not embalmed according to the manner of the Egyptians. The body was wrapped in half-dressed deer skins; at its feet lay a pair of moccasins, and various trinkets and ornaments, such as were worn by the Aborigines. Human bones have been dug up in different parts of the cave, and numerous Indian relics and curiosities found; such as bows, arrow-heads, hatchets, and other articles of Indian warfare. Near a place called Richardson's Spring is a rock in which the prints of moccasins are distinctly visible, suggesting the interesting probability of the cave having been, at some remote period, inhabited by "a race of forest-born monarchs."

We are now upon the high bank above the River Styx, celebrated in Mammoth Cave history, as well as in heathen mythology, and from the unearthly darkness and gloom overshadowing it one might almost imagine it to be the fabled stream whose name it bears. We descend a long sloping bank to the water's edge. Huge defiant-looking rocks overarch the entrance. Beyond and below is chaos. Our dim lights will not penetrate the profound darkness, which hangs like a pall before us. We enter a small boat; our lamps are placed in the bottom, so that the light will be reflected upwards, and we are launched upon the inky bosom of these ever midnight waters. Gradually the light falls upon the broad, finely arched ceiling, beneath which we are noiselessly gliding— with occasional fissures in the rock, revealing the intense darkness beyond. Our Charon, with his dark luminous eyes peering from under his slouched hat, as he sits crouched in the stern of the boat, presents a highly imaginative picture of his fabulous namesake. It was a fine scene for a crayon.

A third of a mile carries us to the opposite shore. After a short walk over rocks and sandbanks, we come to another boat of larger dimensions, which is to bear us over the waters of Lethe. We are now three hundred and twenty-five feet below the surface of the earth. This river sometimes rises fifty feet above its present height; and with its foaming cataracts, and its yawning chasms gurgling with the sound of rushing water, is said to present an aspect of awful grandeur.

This passage is nearly a mile long, and the whole distance replete with interest. At the further end is the famous Echo River, which during high water is merely a continuance of Lethe. The entrance to this river is through an arched gateway of rocks, so low that a slight rise of the water will prevent the passage of boats, and at no time is there a space of more than three feet between the water and the rocks above. We were fortunate in finding sufficient space to admit our boat; although for a few moments we were compelled to *humble* ourselves in a manner neither graceful nor agreeable.

This ordeal passed, we emerged into the open river, where the rocks were high above our heads. While here, our guide fired a pistol, the report of which was deafening. The sound reverberated and echoed from arch to arch, and dome to dome, like continuous thunder. The echo is truly wonderful, and answers fully the descriptions that have been given of it, continuing, I should judge, for some twelve or fifteen seconds. At first, it is remarkably clear and distinct, but changes to a soft and musical cadence as it dies away in the distance. I notified Stephen the night before, when I engaged him to go with us into the cave, that he must be prepared to do justice to his reputation as a singer, as we should expect him to "discourse most eloquent music" on the occasion.

It is a fact known to all who are familiar with this part of the cave, that sound is very much modified and softened by being produced here; while, at the same time, the volume is greatly increased. The harshest notes become quite mellow, and the most unmelodious voices comparatively sweet. It is not strange then, that Stephen, who has a rich, musical voice, and a thorough knowledge of acoustics in its connexion with this place, should prove an attractive feature in the scene. He sang for us several popular airs appropriate to the occasion—such as "The Canadian Boat Song," "My old Kentucky Home," and "Oft in the Stilly Night." He would pause long enough at the end of every line, for the *last word* to be echoed back, the effect of which was indescribably fine. In the song of "Oft in the Stilly Night," the word *night* came back clear and distinct, and as musical as

> "———a heavenly breath
> Along an earthly lyre."

There was a pathos blended and infused into the melody, which caused a feeling of sadness to steal imperceptibly over me. While impressed with these feelings, Stephen commenced singing "Old Hundred," assisted by Mr. Frazer, whose voice was exceedingly rich and powerful. It was impressive beyond description, and I almost imagined myself in some vast cathedral, listening to the rich swelling notes of the organ. A change came over the spirit of my dreams, I was no longer of this "earth, earthy," but an inhabitant of the celestial world. I was transferred, in imagination, to the abodes of bliss—to the midnight sanctuary of the Great Jehovah—where the air was vocal with the swelling notes of Praise from his attendant choir of angels.

> "For *what* can wake
> The soul's strong instinct of another world,
> Like music!"

We are now "on the other side of" Lethe, and I am not forgetful that we have yet five weary miles "over a hard road to travel," before we reach the further end of this universe of wonders. The scenery has entirely changed. Our path is constantly obstructed by fragmentary rocks, over which we climb; chasms, into which we descend; and wild unearthly places, through which we pass: and were it not for the grandeur of the scene, and the visions of sandwiches and other edibles promised at the end, constantly before me, I could not have accomplished the distance without the friendly aid of Stephen's back, which has been a "pack-saddle" for many a valetudinarian, whose curiosity was greater than his endurance. But Stephen promises us new sights and new marvels, and I must try and follow him.

As my sheet is becoming longer, I fear, than your patience, I shall only describe a few of the preminent attractions of this five miles of wonders. We pass *through* Silliman's Avenue, two miles in length, and *over* the Infernal Regions, which are almost as deep, and finally reach the Pass of El Ghor—a fearful-looking place a mile and a half long, which is filled with enormous rocks above, below, and around, looking as if the least jar would dislodge and hurl them upon our devoted heads. As we climbed over the immense boulders which appeared as if they had just fallen from the roof, and gazed for the first time on the dark Titanic masonry rising on each side a hundred feet above us; with its fearful looking clefts, its yawning seams, and ponderous masses of loosened rock staring us in the face, it was not strange that "each particular hair" of our heads should incline to a perpendicular attitude. And when I beheld an enormous rock projecting over us like "a mighty Atlantean roof," without any visible support, I confess that I became insensible to fatigue, and my locomotion was quickened into increased activity until I was beyond the reach of all imaginary danger.

After climbing over a few more rocks, and passing through several narrow defiles, we reached the terminus of this truly perilous-looking labyrinth. A long ladder invited us to ascend. On reaching the top, we found ourselves within a bower worthy of being dedicated to the Goddess Pomona. It is called Martha's Vineyard, on account of the beautiful incrustations, resembling in form and appearance immense bunches of grapes, which cluster upon its sides and ceiling. These pearl-tinted and amber-hued products of this subterranean vineyard are beautiful to look at, and would be likely to excite the alimentiveness and cupidity of some of the fair daughters of Eve, were their curiosity as irrepressible as that of their great ancestress. But this calcareous fruit, I imagine, would not be very palatable; or the tasting of it as productive of serious consequences to after-humanity, as was the eating the product of "the forbidden tree" by our first parents.

After leaving this bower, we entered a long avenue, and a short walk brought us to Washington Hall, the usual place for dining; and from the quantities of broken bottles scattered around and other *spiritual* manifestations, I judged that many of the visitors, if not converts to spiritualism, were at least desirous to cultivate an intimate acquaintance with that recondite subject. We rested here for a while, ate our biscuit and ham (without champagne sauce), and "talked turkey" over the dissected limb of a venerable gobbler, whose toughness was as incredible as his age.

The next place worthy of note is Cleveland's Avenue, which many consider to be one of the principal attractions of this cavernous temple. It is a gorgeous apartment, rivalling in beauty the Gothic avenue, though much more extensive. This avenue is three miles long, about twenty feet high, and from sixty to seventy feet wide; its vast ceiling and sides are covered with white crystallizations, studded with stalactical gems, and sparkling with calcareous diamonds. It has been said by a distinguished geologist, that this avenue contains a petrified form of nearly every vegetable production indigenous to this locality. There is undoubtedly some truth in this assertion, for the walls and ceiling are covered with incrustations resembling in shape and appearance many kinds of vegetables, fruits, and flowers. Some of these are massive in their proportions, and hard as adamant; others, small and delicate as the lily, and fragile as wax-work. "So exquisite and beautiful," says one tourist, "is Cleveland's Avenue, that it is out of the power of painter or poet to conceive anything like it. Such loveliness cannot, indeed, be described. —Were the sovereigns of wealthy states to spend their all on the most skilful lapidaries they could find, with the view of rivalling the splendor of this truly regal abode, the attempt would be entirely in vain. * * *

"It is incrusted from end to end with the most beautiful formations, in every variety of form. The base of the whole is carbonate of lime—in one part of dazzling whiteness, and perfectly smooth; and in other places, crystallized so as to glitter like diamonds in the light.

"Some of the crystals bear a striking resemblance to branches of celery, and all are about the same length, while others, a foot or more in length, have the color and appearance of vanilla cream candy. Others are set in sulphate of lime, in the form of a rose; and others still roll out from the base in forms resembling the ornaments on the capital of a Corinthian column. Some of the incrustations are massive and splendid; others are as delicate as the lily, or as fancy-work of shell or wood. Let any person think of traversing an arched way like this for a mile and a half, and all the wonders of the tales of youth— not forgetting those gorgeous fictions, 'The Arabian Nights'—seem tame and uninteresting when brought into comparison with the living, growing reality. The term 'growing' is not a misnomer; the process is going on before your eyes. Successive coats of these incrustations have been perfected, and then crowded off by others; so that hundreds of tons of these gems lie at your feet, and are crushed as you pass, while the work of restoring the ornaments for Nature's *boudoir* is proceeding around you. Here and there through the whole extent, you will find openings in the side, into which you may thrust the person, and often stand erect in little grottoes, perfectly incrusted with a delicate white substance, reflecting the lights from a thousand glittering points. Many visitors are so enraptured with the place, that they cannot repress exclamations of surprise or worship."

We will now leave this avenue. A short walk brings us to the Rocky Mountains, "the *fourth* and last" great feature of this subterranean universe. I hardly know how to describe the awful grandeur of this place, and its adjunct, The Dismal Hollow. It is a room of immense breadth and height, with a mountainous pile of rocks at its entrance, which rise in the form of an amphitheatre nearly to the ceiling. These rocks are of almost every conceivable size and form; sharp, jagged, and heaped together in "chaotic confusion," having undoubtedly been loosened from the roof by some tremendous convulsion of Nature. Clambering up this mountain of rocks fifty or sixty feet, we discovered on the other side an immense hollow stretching off into the darkness and gloom. Our guide illuminated the place, revealing the wilderness of desolation before us. You can conceive of nothing terrestrial that is more dismal and sepulchral than this spot, which impressed us with a kind of "holy horror" as we gazed into its gloomy confines.

A short distance from here is Croghan's Hall, the end of this portion of the cave, and nine miles from *daylight*, and "the light of other days." This is a large room, semi-rotunda in form, the roof and sides of which are draped with wavy sheets of stalactite, extending from the ceiling to the floor. Some were a dingy white, others of a translucent, icy hue, looking not unlike a congealed water-fall. In the dim distance, uprising from the rocky floor, were several stalagmite columns, about the size of the human form; which, amid the sepulchral stillness of this weird-like place, looked as if they might be sheeted ghosts or "goblins damn'd." While gazing on these apparitions there came over me—

"An undefined and sudden thrill
That makes the heart a moment still,
Then beat with quicker pulse, ashamed
Of that strange sense of silence framed."

While my imagination was thus excited, our guide extinguished the lamps, and led us slowly along through the intense darkness which enveloped us like a pall. I had great confidence in Stephen, yet I could not divest myself of a sort of nervous apprehension and dread, as we followed him with slow and cautious footsteps. After proceeding quite a distance he stopped and ignited a Bengal light. As the blue sulphurous flame ascended, I discovered that we were standing on the brink of a frightful abyss. I started back alarmed, but being reassured by our guide, approached this yawning chasm. As I looked down into its fearful depths, which had never yet been fathomed, my ear was greeted by the dull roar of an invisible waterfall. The ground was damp and slippery, from a mist, which, though scarcely perceptible, was diffused through the surrounding atmosphere. A kind of nervous chillness crept over me, and I instinctively shuddered as I gazed into these gloomy regions. It was by far the most frightful place I ever beheld, and I could hardly realize that I was not standing on the brink of that mythical place known as Tartarus; which has been described as

"A black and hollow vault
Where day is never seen; there shines no sun,
But flaming horror of consuming fires;
A lightless sulphur, chok'd with smoky fogs
Of an infected darkness."

A thousand fantasies filled my mind, and I was glad to leave this place of supernatural horrors, lest my sleep that night be disturbed by spectral visions and apparitions dire.

On our return voyage of the Lethe, we tried to catch some of the eyeless fish which abound in that river, but the water was too deep for success. As I did not have the pleasure of seeing one of these anomalies of the finny tribe, I shall have to depend for a description upon those who have been more fortunate than myself. They are about the size of a minnow, from one and a half to two inches long, perfectly white, translucent, and without a vestige of the visual organ. Scientific men, however, disagree in this particular. Some say that they cannot discover the least appearance of an eye, even with a powerful microscope; while others contend that they once had eyes, and that a collapsed socket is clearly discernible. But when learned men disagree upon piscatory subjects, who is to of-*fish*-iate as umpire?

How I got back to the "breathing world" again to dinner and daylight, I have not time now to inform you. Though I had performed a journey of eighteen miles, in and out, within a period of nine hours, I resolved to add one more mile to my day's labor, and visit again the Star Chamber, to take one "long, last, lingering look" at this brilliantly beautiful apartment, and to gaze for a while upon those *midnight sentinels* in the glorious firmament above—upon the stars, those silent spirits of Nature, though *silent* they seem,

> " Yet each to the thoughtful eye,
>   Glows with *mute poesy !*"

My companion from the land of Burns—who had lived for many years among the " banks and braes o' Bonnie Doon"—was of a highly poetical temperament, and, like the immortal bard, an enthusiastic admirer of Nature. I was glad to find that he was desirous, like myself, to revisit this attractive spot, to behold once more this glorious evidence of God's omnipotence. We seated ourselves on a rock, and gave our lamps to Stephen, who was to leave us alone for a while, that we might the better enjoy the solemn silence of this vast cathedral of Nature. When the last footfall had died on the ear, and the last gleam of light disappeared, we found ourselves plunged suddenly into Cimmerian darkness. Hark! let pulse and breath be still! We could not speak. Our thoughts were too deep for utterance: our wonder and amazement too great for expression. It seemed as if I never before felt so impressively the majesty and goodness of the Creator of all this grandeur. We were aroused from our reverie by the resounding footsteps of our guide, and the gradual lightening up of the grim grey walls surrounding us. The illusory sky appeared to our view, with its twinkling stars and passing cloud, and we left this soul-absorbing spot with reluctance and regret. * * * * *

From the geological formation of this cave, and other indications observed by visitors in their examinations, it is evident that it contains many apartments that have not yet been explored. In several places the hollow floor echoes and resounds at our tread, and we are doubtless passing over some vast cavern or opening underneath, separated from the room above by a thin layer of rock. And in one or more places where there is a slight opening, the sound of an invisible waterfall may be heard, roaring and tumbling in its frantic but vain efforts to be released from captivity.

In the vicinity of the Mammoth Cave, are several smaller caves already explored; also, indications of there being many others, to which, as yet, there is no entrance from the upper world. The whole of this region is cavernous, and abounds in pits or "sinks" as they are called, where the surface of the earth has sunk to various depths, indicating the existence of a cavity beneath.

What magnificent Halls, Domes, and Avenues, decorated with as brilliant stalactites, as beautiful crystallizations, and as rare mineralogical specimens as the eye ever beheld, lie concealed beneath these hills and valleys, it remains perhaps for the future to disclose. It is a fruitful theme for the imagination. Its revelations—if its hidden mysteries are ever to be revealed, are reserved for the future discoverer; and its history—if ever to be written—to the historian of after time.

THE END.

www.ingramcontent.com/pod-product-compliance
Lightning Source LLC
Chambersburg PA
CBHW030746230426
43667CB00007B/865